Coaching Outside the Box

Changing the Mindset in Youth Soccer

Volume I

By Paul S.A. Mairs and Richard E. Shaw

Edited by

Anthony W. Annunziata Ph.D.

D1385374

Mairs & Shaw Publishing
Syracuse, New York

Coaching Outside the Box: Changing the Mindset in Youth Soccer Volume I

Copyright © 2012 by Paul S.A. Mairs and Richard E. Shaw

Mairs, Paul S.A.

Shaw, Richard E.

Coaching Outside the Box: Changing the Mindset in Youth Soccer Volume I

ISBN-13: 978-0615700120
ISBN-10: 0615700128

Mairs & Shaw Publishing
Syracuse, New York

www.mairsandshaw.com

Contents

The Authors

Richard Shaw

 Growing up in North West England, Richard was surrounded by soccer from an early age. His playing career began during his early years at school, and by the age of 10 he was invited to join the youth system at Blackpool FC based in his hometown of Blackpool, Lancashire.

At 16, Blackpool FC offered him a two year YTS contract, so he graduated high school, signed with the club and began training and playing fulltime. During this time Richard played with some of England's best upcoming players while facing the youth teams of clubs such as Manchester United, Manchester City, and Liverpool FC. Additionally, he made several reserve team appearances and was selected for the first team squad just before his 18th birthday.

After spending a total of 8 years at Blackpool FC, Richard moved on to Kendal Town FC where he spent two years. At this point he became interested in coaching, and while gaining experience working with young players in local schools he completed his UEFA Coaching license through the PFA (Professional Footballer's Association). He was also invited by Blackpool FC's youth academy director (Wayne Harrison) to work with the U9's and presented with an opportunity to travel to the U.S. to coach in Minnesota.

After enjoying his experiences in America, he decided to pursue college playing opportunities, and landed in Syracuse, NY where he played for Bryant and Stratton and for Lemoyne College. During this time, he won a NJCAA Division I National Championship, was awarded All-American honors, and named MVP three consecutive years.

After graduating with a Bachelor's degree in Information Systems, Richard spent the majority of his time furthering his education in youth soccer development. In 2003, he developed a curriculum with his colleague and co-author of this book, Paul Mairs, and it was first implemented by a youth soccer program in New York State.

As the program developed and the curriculum began to have a positive impact on hundreds of young players throughout Central New York, he sat down with Chris Pelligra *(the Director of Operations),* and together they formed NY Soccer Central, a youth soccer program training players aged 5 – 18 which focuses on each player's individual development and maintaining their involvement in the sport.

Living in New York State with his wife Elizabeth, Richard continued his playing career after signing professionally with the Syracuse Silver Knights of the MISL (Major Indoor Soccer League); he remains heavily involved in youth development and enjoys working with Time Warner Sports as a soccer analyst and commentator.

Paul Mairs

Paul also grew up in Blackpool and from an early age displayed a strong appetite for the sport, starting at the age of 5 with a local youth soccer club. By age 11, Paul was invited to train with the youth system of local professional soccer team Blackpool Football Club.

At the age of 14, Paul was selected to play for the Lancashire Schoolboys, and while captaining the team he attracted interest from a number of English Premier League clubs, most notably Wimbledon FC and Leeds United AFC.

After receiving an offer from Wimbledon Football Club, Paul opted to sign his first contract at only 16 years of age with Blackpool FC and trained with the club every day for the next two years. During this time Paul made a number of reserve team appearances and was also selected in the first team squad several times.

After spending seven years at the club, Paul continued his career playing semi-professionally for various clubs in North West England. During this time Paul also undertook his Football Association (FA) coaching qualifications and travelled regularly to the U.S to help develop a curriculum with his colleague Richard Shaw. In 2006, Paul graduated with a Bachelor's degree in sports studies and coaching, and later graduated with a Master's degree in Sport Management from the University of Central Lancashire.

Over the past decade, Paul has worked in sports development and has continued to help progress coaching methods and curriculums for various organizations both in the U.S. and U.K. In order to gain further understanding of applied physiological and psychological aspects of sports performance, he embarked on a sport science degree with Manchester Metropolitan University in 2010, sponsored by the Professional Footballer's Association. Paul currently resides in the North of England and is now a running enthusiast taking part in marathons in numerous countries.

Foreword

Richard Shaw and Paul Mairs have a great passion concerning youth development in sport; they believe the vehicle of sport can move mountains in the minds of young people. Handled correctly it can improve the person and the talent, but handled incorrectly only negative results will follow. They dispute and debate the rights and wrongs of correct youth development in soccer like a lioness reproaching her cubs; ferocity and drive for this protection of their favorite sport is limitless and no stone is left unturned.

Anyone who cares to listen can only become more informed and educated. This book radiates Richard and Paul's passion and expertly advises those who want to listen about the simplicity of doing things right, after all the beautiful game is not 'rocket science' but merely simplicity personified, only made complicated by adults.

Children are not mini-adults; they are children, both intriguing and innocent and there is not one like the other, and all respond differently at various stages of development. Each child has to be allowed the freedom of expression and the right to learn from mistakes; most importantly they must be allowed to have fun and play, as children have done since the dawn of time. Tony Whelan the Head of Academy Coaching at Manchester United Football Club consistently reminds us as coaches that children only have one childhood and it's our privilege to be part of that childhood; therefore as custodians we cannot fail them.

After well over a decade working with elite young players, I'm fully aware that many aspiring Ronaldo's' will not realize the dream of becoming a professional soccer player; this befalls to a rare few. As a coach then, it is even more imperative that the majority who don't 'reach the stars' have a good time in trying to get as far as they possibly can. The aim of any coach should be about their players developing a lifelong love for the game within a nurturing and calm environment, which is both holistic and balanced. Only a developmental philosophy will work in the end and this book exhibits ways in which to provide one.

Dean Whitehouse - BA with honors, and MSc.
Manchester United Youth Academy Coach

Acknowledgements

First, we would like to thank Professor Annunziata for his work and time editing this material. He made the process smooth and enjoyable.

Additionally, for his valuable insight, energy, and providing us with the opportunity to spend time at Manchester United's training facility we would like to thank Dean Whitehouse.

We would also like to offer our appreciation to John Allpress, Rick Fenoglio, John Hills, Professor James Mandingo, and Daniel Massaro as well as the numerous elite coaches, development experts, and researchers who have provided us with excellent resources while preparing this material.

Paul would like to thank all of his family for their patience during the last three years. This book would not have been possible without their support.

Richard thanks his amazing wife and family for always being there. He also thanks those parents who displayed patience and trust with the development of their children over the years.

"Our present educational system and social conditioning powerfully conform. The individual is taught from the earliest age to surrender himself or herself to the team. Nothing is more sternly rebuked than self-assertion at the expense of group achievement. No one is more praised than the good team player; none is more reviled than the individual who pursues his own goals."[1]

John Galbraith *- Advisor to former President John F Kennedy*

"Whenever you find that you are on the side of the majority, it is time to pause and reflect."[2]

Mark Twain - *American author and humorist*

Before we start

Over the last 25 years we have gained significant insight as our playing careers progressed from the youth levels through to the college and professional ranks of the game. As youth coaches, we have also had the opportunity to work with many clubs, coaches, families, and young players of all ages both in the U.S. and U.K. Furthermore, we have undertaken considerable amounts of research, including extensive travel throughout North America and Europe where we have observed numerous games and training sessions at various levels from U.S. club soccer to some of Europe's leading academies.

From these experiences and observations, and specifically those during the last decade in the U.S., it has become obvious that there is currently a **huge problem in U.S. youth soccer**. The problem is that large numbers of young players encounter negative experiences during the early stages of their development **(which we will always refer to as the ages of 5-13 in this book)** and simply are not offered the chance to develop a passion for the sport or the opportunity to unlock their true potential. This is primarily due to a vast majority of clubs, coaches, and parents involved in youth soccer harboring a conventional mindset, which is underpinned by an insatiable appetite for **winning, instantaneous gratification, and a premature focus on what is best for the team instead of focusing on the development of each individual player.**

For many this short-sighted approach in youth sport seems quite customary and benign due to societal values and beliefs. Unfortunately, they fail to understand that this obsession for winning and instant fulfillment creates many negative issues detrimental to the young players' experiences and development. Consequently, whether it is intentional or unintentional, coaches and parents often hijack young players' involvement, and what should be a healthy opportunity for children to learn and have fun invariably turns into a situation where the adults' emotions and feelings inappropriately take center stage.

As we reveal in this book by analyzing some basic issues and concepts in each chapter, this conventional mindset involves coaches and parents repetitively demonstrating misguided actions and frequently regurgitating outdated beliefs, ideas, and methods. Researchers Professor Mark Williams and Dr. Nicola Hodges support this viewpoint in their study investigating practice and skill acquisition in soccer by stating, "Current coaching practice is determined mainly by subjective evidence and the historical precedence established within the club, what others have referred to as the processes of intuition, tradition and emulation **rather than on empirical evidence.**"[3]

As these coaches and parents rarely take a moment to reflect upon their behavior and are simply not conscious of the negative ramifications that surface through their actions and beliefs, **young players are placed in unhealthy situations.** When discussing this issue and more specifically the win-at-all-cost mentality during players' formative years, Sam Snow, the U.S. Youth Soccer Director, refers to it as, **"An American disease."**[4] It is no wonder why our very own director refers to this in such a harsh manner when we consider that an astounding **70% to 80% of kids stop playing soccer after the age of 12.**[5]

Although we must acknowledge that there may be other reasons why some children cease to participate at such a young age, there can be no doubt that the conventional approach taken by so many clubs, coaches, and parents is the major driver behind this truly worrying drop out statistic. As editor of the NSCAA Soccer Journal, Dr. J Martin points out, **"The number one reason they stop playing is that they are no longer having fun. That is a real problem."**[6] This is supported by Dr. Robert Weinberg and Professor Daniel Gould in their publication <u>Foundations of Sports and Exercise Psychology</u>. They affirm that a high number of young players cite factors related to the negative aspects of the conventional approach as influencing their decision to withdraw from the sport. These factors include a lack of enjoyment, low perceived competence, excessive pressure, a dislike of the coach, and crucially an **overemphasis on winning** and **short-term outcomes.**[7]

This problem is accurately summarized by Fred Engh, author and president of the National Alliance for Youth Sports, who substantiates that it is adults who are primarily responsible for this disturbing outcome:

Studies show that an alarming <u>70% of the approximately 20 million children</u> who participate in organized out-of-school athletic programs will quit by the age of thirteen because of **unpleasant sports experiences**. That's 17.5 million unhappy, dispirited children. It's a frightening statistic that paints a rather bleak picture of organized sports in America today. The culprits are the adults who, in their roles as coaches, administrators, and parents, **have misguided motives and ideals of what youth sports are all about.**[8]

Professor Frank Smoll and his colleagues also expose how this winning mentality is completely misguided and destructive for young players' early experiences and development:

> The common notion in sports equates success with victory. However, with a 'winning is everything philosophy', young athletes lose opportunities to develop their skills, to enjoy their participation, and to grow socially and emotionally.[9]

Additionally, leading developmental expert and sports psychologist Rainer Martens, who has written extensively for the last three decades on a number of integral issues and concepts related to youth sport, further substantiates all these viewpoints by condemning this win-at-all-cost mentality:

> Society seems to indicate that it values winning more than development because it clearly rewards winners. That message, however, as powerful as it is, is sent by misguided rascals who do not understand the deeper meaning of sport in our society. **It's a message you must reject.**[10]

In light of so many developmental experts strongly opposing the conventional approach and the remarkable dropout figures in youth soccer, one can see that there is an **urgent need** for people to abandon their current way of thinking. But changing the mindset is certainly going to be a challenging task due to the fact that many coaches and parents are **unaware** that a major problem in youth soccer even exists and that there are alternative methods which provide young people with better experiences and developmental opportunities.

The difficulty of this task significantly increases as many self-proclaimed leading clubs operating throughout the U.S. declare that their main objective is primarily on the long-term development of their players, but yet do everything in their power to put together winning teams even at the youngest age groups and ruthlessly sacrifice young players' experiences and development in pursuit of this objective.

We find it remarkable and very concerning that many of these clubs are trusted by parents for the care and well-being of their children and paid significant fees for their services and so called 'professionalism', yet their actions and beliefs evidently conflict the opinions of numerous developmental experts, elite coaches working at Europe's best academies, **and their very own U.S. Directors Sam Snow and Claudio Reyna.** Although these key figures continually attempt to make a positive difference by encouraging clubs and coaches to embrace new ideas in order to **truly** place the emphasis on player development, these self-proclaimed leading clubs unwaveringly march on with their outdated philosophies and methods, doing whatever it takes to accumulate as many trophies as possible during the early stages of players' development. **But why is this happening?**

Either these self-affirmed leading clubs are completely unacquainted with the views of developmental experts and their national directors concerning what it takes to truly guide and nurture young players in the sport, or they are deliberately choosing to ignore this information because they harbor ulterior motives. Evidence strongly suggests that it is the latter, as a high percentage of these clubs post numerous models, articles, and pdf files on their websites which support a 'long-term' developmental approach and **oppose the conventional methods they actually implement.**

For example, a self-proclaimed leading club based in Central New York had an insightful article linked to their website discussing the problems of tournaments and **young players travelling excessive amounts** to attend them. The article argued how young players should spend more time focusing on their individual development and less time taking part in events that are damaging to their welfare and progress in the sport. Interestingly, the document quoted Bobby Howe, the former Director of Coaching for the United States Soccer Federation, stressing "There is no need for players under the age of 13 to play out of state."[11] In spite of the fact that this club was advocating this article on their website, their homepage was a celebration of how their U11 Boys just won a tournament in Maryland. Furthermore, it boastfully announced how they were off to Virginia next weekend to compete in another tournament!

This is just one example of many where clubs **contradict themselves** and their claimed philosophy, and simply go against what leading figures advocate. But did not one coach or administrator involved with the club recognize that they were transmitting mixed messages via their website and making themselves look foolish by promoting an out of state tournament win while providing **compelling evidence** that they should not be doing it in the first place? Maybe clubs employing this tactic are just hoping it goes under the radar. Regardless, this strongly suggests that many clubs ignore the messages of leading figures, and/or post these supportive articles on their websites as a façade in an attempt to appear as though they are focusing primarily on player development when they are **clearly not.**

Of course, many of these clubs are aware that due to misguided perceptions of success a large percentage of parents and players gravitate towards the organizations that have a winning reputation, even at the earliest age groups. We must also remember that many clubs are driven by a desire to increase revenue. Therefore, by dismissing the thoughts of developmental experts and placing the primary focus on winning at all costs while promoting the accumulation of trophies and tournament success, these clubs increase their chances of enticing parents and players into their program and thus increasing the number of paying customers. We call this state of affairs **'business before development'**, and with it is always the overriding philosophy of **'what young players can do for the club, instead of what the club can do for young players'.**

Regardless of the reasons why one takes this conventional approach in youth soccer, after constantly being in environments and observing so many clubs, coaches, and parents demonstrating inappropriate actions, and importantly identifying how this negatively impacts young players, we felt compelled to write this book. Essentially, we aspire to make a positive difference by helping more young players receive effective guidance through convincing more coaches and parents to adopt a **developmental and healthier outlook** in youth soccer. This in turn will undoubtedly encourage more players to remain in the sport which should always be the true measurement of success.

We are optimistic in reaching this objective because we have been able to successfully implement the concepts in this book which truly facilitate individual player development and place winning and team success on the back burner until players reach their later teenage years. Furthermore, due to our continuous work and persistence in educating coaches and parents about the need to embrace a developmental approach towards youth soccer, we have been encouraged greatly as many have discarded their old ways of thinking and embraced a more positive outlook which has been far more beneficial for everyone. Our program is firsthand proof that the ideals and perspectives of leading figures and experts are legitimate and powerful; if one has the courage and conviction to stand up and go against the grain, then these ideals can be implemented to great effect.

There can be no doubt that having an open mind and recognizing the fact that we are always learning has allowed our organization to move in the right direction. But as our philosophy toward development has been and remains to be strongly opposed by many non-reflective people, we have faced resistance and obstructions along the way. Frustratingly, some problems have come from the parents whose children we are trying to help as they have frequently demonstrated misguided perspectives on development in youth sport.

Although a high number of parents involved in our organization support our developmental approach, there are those who have succumbed to false information and have simply been deceived by clubs and coaches only concerned about winning and short-term accolades. Consequently, some

parents have unwisely chosen to take their child into unhealthy environments. We are pleased to say that this has only been a small minority of the families that we have been involved with over the years.

We have also found that a good percentage of parents who choose to subject their child to an environment where the conventional approach is taken swiftly remove them once they establish that the club they've joined is only concerned with **what their child could do for them, instead of what the club can do for their child.** Many of these returning parents also shared accounts of how their child had encountered a bad experience or that the promises that these clubs utilized to entice them were merely fabrications.

Determined to take the right approach and truly focus on the players' best interests, we have seen this positively impact the lives and experiences of numerous young people in Central New York. Many of these individuals who have trained consistently in our development program have progressed to become very effective soccer players in their **later teens**. And all of these players display a natural competitive edge which so many coaches and parents in youth soccer assume only comes from repeatedly traveling out of state to face the 'best competition' during the players' formative years. This experience alone demonstrates that consistently travelling far and wide with the youngest of players in search of highly competitive opponents and contests is not necessary *(hence why it is opposed by so many leading figures in the game, something we will expose further later in this book).*

The steady progress of players in our program has allowed many of them to pursue college playing careers. This substantiates that we are taking an effective approach during their early years. But what we regard as our greatest achievement is how we have encouraged many young players to maintain their passion for the sport and stay involved in the game; and for many the signs look promising that their passion will be a lifelong one.

For children to be captivated by the sport, it is absolutely imperative that their initial experiences are stimulating, enjoyable, and educational. Winning must always take a backseat to development during these crucial years. In their book, <u>Youth Soccer: From Science to Performance</u>, Professor Gareth Stratton and his colleagues remind us of what the true objectives in youth soccer should really be, "Programs for soccer have two major goals: The first is to engage players in lifelong participation in the sport; and the second is to maintain a professional outlook that continues to aspire and motivate youngsters to participate."[12]

What is this book going to do?

Our objective is to change the current mindset and conventional approach in U.S youth soccer. We believe that by highlighting some key issues and altering the way that coaches and parents think about them is going to allow us to make a major change in the overall psyche.

The issues we discuss are straightforward concepts which we have broken down to illustrate why the conventional approach is so harmful for many young players and makes no sense from a developmental perspective. However, when these issues are eliminated and alternative methods are implemented during the players' formative years, we demonstrate how it has a positive impact on their experiences and progress.

So, if you are a parent with a child involved in youth soccer, the information in this book will be **powerful,** and it will positively impact your perspectives, your child's experiences, and their long-term progress. After reading through the chapters, you will be able to identify **what coaches should and should not be doing when working with any young players between the ages of 5-13**. Furthermore, you will be able to recognize whether the club or organization you are involved in is truly focusing on players' best interests or whether they have alternative motives.

Equally, if you are a youth soccer coach *at any level* who is **truly** focused on helping young players ignite a passion for the game while unlocking their true potential, the guidance and evidence presented in this book will help you achieve these objectives and allow you to become a more effective coach, as all the information is validated by elite coaches, developmental experts, and empirical research. This book also demonstrates how coaches do not need to be highly qualified or have advanced understanding of tactical components of the game to ensure that **young players** are provided with a positive learning environment. There are far more important coaching prerequisites when working with young children such as a **calm temperament, a caring nature, a positive outlook, and the ability to constantly reflect upon one's actions**.

For those clubs, coaches, and parents obsessed with immediate success and trophy accumulation during the early stages of development, **this book has the potential to cause problems**, as there will be a strong possibility that you will be held accountable for your misguided actions by people who read this material. Undoubtedly, the information in this book will expose any incompetence, ignorance, or misleading behavior demonstrated by any organization or individual, and it will encourage many people to **ask questions and demand answers**.

We strive to convince more clubs, coaches, and parents to have the courage and integrity to reflect upon on their actions and make the changes so desperately needed to benefit young players' experiences, welfare, and development. Once more people take this path, the chances will certainly increase of retaining higher numbers in the sport and developing more effective soccer players in the long-term, which from both perspectives can only be positive for soccer in the U.S.

Coaching Outside the Box: Changing the Mindset in Youth Soccer

Chapter One

Approach to Games

"As adults, we can choose to structure events and contests so that competition is a learning experience. Competition becomes negative when winning becomes the overriding goal. In these instances, the majority of individuals will feel beaten and defeated."[13]

Karen Hinton – Former Dean, University of Nevada

Games provide young players with powerful learning opportunities that are essential for their progress and enjoyment in the sport.[14] As we will reveal, developmental experts and elite coaches working at leading professional academies throughout the world fully understand this principle and therefore **utilize games primarily for learning during the early stages of development**. But as we outlined in 'Before we Start', the majority of organizations, coaches, and parents involved in U.S. youth soccer adopt a **win-at-all-cost mentality** and games represent the big stage where the most important factor is outdoing the opposition. As a result, many youngsters are simply **cheated out of the opportunity to learn, experiment, and maximize their enjoyment during games.** This will become much clearer in the following chapters as we examine some key issues in close detail. But to get us started, we are simply going to demonstrate the contrasting nature of these two approaches.

First, what we see consistently throughout the youth soccer landscape are games being frequently overhyped and turned into highly charged spectacles where coaches and parents, *consciously or not,* shape the young players' mind that 'success' is judged primarily on the end result of the game. For example, the traditional pre-game 'pep talk' exemplifies this state of affairs. We have observed many coaches and parents accentuating the game result just before kickoff *(especially when the opposition is a perceived 'rival')* and completely neglecting any notion of learning and enjoyment in the process. For example, we commonly hear coaches making comments to their young players such as:

- *"Last time we played these guys they beat us. We owe them!"*

- *"Watch out for number 9 - he's very dangerous! If we let him shoot, we'll pay the price!"*

- *"You must bring your 'A' game today if we're gonna beat these guys!!!"*

- *"If you're not working hard for the team, I'll take you off the field!"*

- *"We've got to be physical out there today, if we want to win!"*

The customary pre-game 'pep talk' - used inappropriately by many coaches who focus on winning

This perspective where each game is the 'big event' and the score is hugely significant simply leaves many young players feeling encumbered by an intense pressure to perform for coaches and parents in the aim of producing a win. Although this type of pre-game 'pep talk' is robotically implemented by many, it simply distracts players from learning and transmits the message that they are headed off onto the battlefield! But pumping up players before the game in this fashion will often be counterproductive anyway. In order to substantiate this point, Associate Professor Tiffanye Vargas-Tonsing from the University of Texas investigated the effects of coaches' pre-game speeches on young players' perceptions of self-confidence and emotion. She established that taking this approach can push athletes beyond their optimal arousal and towards a performance decline.[15]

Interestingly, if we asked these coaches and parents about the importance of winning, many would play it down and brandish the ever predictable sound bites such as, *"The most important thing is that the children are having fun - it's not that important if they win or lose."* Unfortunately, this philosophy often goes completely 'out the window' as soon as the young players take to the field and adults' emotions spiral out of control. But rather than go into this now, we will save this for later.

Shaping the young players' minds into believing that winning is the ultimate goal and subjecting them to tasks that are geared towards achieving that objective will cause many players to simply focus on what it takes to win the game. This often entails players displaying limited imagination, taking no risks, and attempting no new skills. The following scenario demonstrates this point:

> *Sarah, who is 9 years old, is very fast and can **kick the ball far**. The coach, knowing these strengths, places her on defense and before the game instructs her to kick the ball as hard as she can up to the forwards every time she gets it. Throughout the game she kicks the ball forward many times, creating chances for her forwards to go through on goal. However, she rarely looks where or whom she is kicking the ball to, and never attempts to beat an opponent by dribbling or executing a creative piece of skill. Toward the end of the game, the ball comes to her, and instead of just kicking the ball up the field one more time, she attempts to control it, but fails to keep possession and the opposing player steals the ball and almost scores. The coach screams out to Sarah, **"Don't play with the ball at the back; just kick it up the field! Remember what your job is!"***

In this situation the coach is encouraging Sarah to get the ball forward as soon as she gets it so the attacking players can go through on goal and the danger of losing the ball in the defensive area is decreased. In the early age groups of youth soccer, this tactic is often prevalent as it helps coaches obtain winning results. But let's ask which would be better for Sarah's development as a player: Blasting the ball up the field without much consideration or controlling the ball while working on dribbling and finding accurate passes to her team mates?

Not content with over-hyping the game prior to kickoff and hijacking learning opportunities during the game, after the final whistle many coaches and parents further inflate the notion that the game result is more important than it actually is. We regularly witness coaches and parents spending significant amounts of time analyzing the performance of the team or individual players. Often coaches sit their team down for long spells on the sidelines after a defeat so they can run through the 'vital moments' of the game. During this process these coaches habitually pinpoint individual players' mistakes and scrutinize what the team could have done to gain the win. It is also common to see parents in the parking lot subjecting their own children to a post-game report of what they should and should not have done, even when it is often the last thing the child wants or needs to hear.

Approaching games with this perspective will often handicap players' immediate enjoyment levels and long-term progress. This point is substantiated by researchers Dr. Luke Sage and Dr. Maria Kavussanu, who investigated goal orientations and motivational settings in youth soccer. These authors conclude that if coaches do not provide an environment where learning and skill development takes precedent, there is a high probability players will lose interest and ultimately drop out of the sport.[16] One can clearly see why this is the case when taking on board the perspectives of Dr. Robert Weinberg and Professor Daniel Gould. In their book <u>Foundations of Sport and Exercise Psychology</u> they stress how allowing young players to believe that winning games is the benchmark of success is a damaging outlook as, **"Young athletes will lose, so when self-evaluation depends on winning and losing, young athletes can develop low self-worth and thus become less likely to continue sport participation."**[17]

When adults start to understand how approaching games with this winning mentality hinders development, it encourages them to alter their views and they begin to appreciate the more important purpose games serve for young players. However, many clubs throughout the nation are not interested in supporting this transition of thinking. Nor are they willing to implement this change themselves. Again, this is because a high percentage of clubs use winning records to entice players into their organization knowing many uninformed parents relate winning to successful coaching.

A great example which exposes this set of circumstances is the situation encountered by a coach we have known for over a decade. With a wealth of coaching experience both in the U.S and internationally he offered us some interesting views he acquired while working at a large youth soccer club in a southern state. Speaking of how he and other coaches within his organization approached games during the early stages of development, he was unequivocal in his assertion:

> The club is pretty clear in their objectives. They want to produce winning teams and win as many trophies as possible, **even with the younger age groups**. They want to appear successful, and they know that many parents will bring their child to their organization if they are producing winning teams. Conversely, if we lose games, especially to local rivals, this often means that players may leave. So in a way, **our hands are tied when it comes to games and player development**, as there are things we could be working on in realistic game situations that we cannot due to the fact that winning is the main objective.

This situation where coaches are pressured to produce wins surfaces in a high number of youth soccer clubs across the nation. Therefore, the 'need to win' is a philosophy that many organizations find **difficult to discard** and is the logical route they adhere to even though it hampers young players' development during their early years in the sport. Because of this state of affairs, the coach who offered us this previous perspective regarding the win-at-all-cost mentality getting in the way of player development wished to remain anonymous. He informed us that if his name was mentioned his club and their administrators would be angry with him as it would expose that their claimed philosophy of **focusing primarily on player development** is untrue.

Due to the amount of clubs and coaches who march on with an ethos where games serve as a means to promote their club's winning reputation instead of affording the perfect opportunity for young players to learn it leads to many key figures in the sport expressing the huge challenge that lies ahead in order to change this mindset. For example, Kelvin Giles, former Head Coach at the famous Australian Institute of Sport points out that:

> We still have a long way to go in convincing those people responsible for the early years of athletic development that the issue is **not about trophy hunting**, but about the laying down of athletic infrastructures that will last a lifetime.[18]

But we are mindful that coaches do not always place the main emphasis on winning just because they are pressured to produce wins by their club or organization. Coaches are often concerned about how **they** are perceived by parents and others within their local community, so it becomes important to them that they appear to be 'successful' by producing a winning team. Additionally, many youth soccer coaches simply believe that producing wins is their main responsibility and are unaware of or do not even consider that games should be utilized primarily with an alternative objective. But some coaches also adopt this approach since it is all they have ever known throughout their personal experiences in sport. Horst Wein who has worked with major European soccer clubs such as Inter Milan, Real Sociedad, and Leeds United FC shares his view on this issue:

> The major obstacle for progress in soccer coaching is the strength of ease and comfort by the coaches. Because of their own inertia or sluggishness, coaches tend to continue with old habits rather than

continually rethinking what has to be done and how. All too often information is used and exercises are applied that have already lost their validity. Many coaches have not even noticed that the information they obtained years before has already diminished in value.[19]

Unfortunately, many adults also mistakenly assume that young players take to the field with winning as their primary focus. This is substantiated by researchers Dr. Sean Cumming and Associate Professor Martha Ewing who assert, **"Many erroneously believe that winning is the number one reason that children want to play sport."**[20] This is interesting, as further studies show that the majority of young people take part in a sport for reasons more important to them than winning. For example, in an overview of youth sports programs in the U.S., researcher Professor Vern Seefeldt and colleagues establish that learning new skills, staying in shape, enjoying the sport, meeting new friends, and doing something they were good at were all put **ahead of winning** by children as their reasons for their participation in a sport.[21]

Furthermore, coaches and parents must be aware that research indicates many of today's elite athletes never approached competition or games when they were young with this short-term outlook that places winning as the primary objective. Dr. Benjamin Bloom's research in elite talent development was retrospectively outlined across the careers of champion athletes. Bloom established that these individuals did not begin their careers emphasizing competitive outcome (i.e., winning medals, defeating others). Instead these champions focused on having fun, learning fundamentals, and being active, and only **in their later stages of development did they approach competition from a more serious perspective.**[22]

When learning is the primary objective

When one adopts a long-term perspective and is truly concerned about player development, games can be utilized as powerful learning tools during the players' formative years. Again, this outlook towards games is one elite youth soccer coaches, developmental experts, and leading figures in the sport recommend, emphasizing that coaches and parents must take this approach if more players are going to develop confidence, enjoy their soccer experiences, continue their involvement, and become more effective players in the future.

As former U.S. Youth National team coach Manfred Schellscheidt says, **"The game is the best teacher."**[23] So rather than viewing games from a standpoint where the final score is the main objective, it is important to appreciate that game situations offer young players the **perfect opportunity** to experiment with new ideas and take risks with new skills in the heat of the moment.

When we were young and we faced the youth teams of leading Premier League clubs in England, whenever we played against Liverpool Football Club, the coaches were supportive of allowing their players the freedom to attempt new skills, because they understood the importance of utilizing games from a learning perspective. From our observations, this clearly elevated their players' self-belief and **this philosophy continued regardless of the score.**

However, approaching games in this manner offers certain challenges. For example, when using games primarily for learning and development, players are attempting to push out the boundaries by implementing new skills and ideas, and consequently, mistakes will occur more frequently. Therefore, the ability to obtain a game winning result can be impacted negatively. Coaches in this scenario have to refrain from getting caught up in the score and must remove any concern of how others, especially those who believe that a winning coach symbolizes a successful one, may perceive them.

Additionally, it is vitally important that coaches also articulate to players and parents that this developmental approach towards games may negatively impact the ability to win in the short-term. For many this can be a difficult perception to embrace. But when the coach transmits the message that players in the long-term will have more passion for the game and be far more competent and competitive because they received plenty of opportunities to practice skills and enhance their game understanding, this often alleviates concern. This brings us to an important point. **Many young players instinctively strive to win, but we must keep this drive under control and in perspective so that the learning process is not compromised. Simply telling young players** that winning is not important could lead them to developing bad habits in the long-term. If players progress into their late teens and then demonstrate the capabilities to play at the college or professional level, it is essential to have a strong competitive drive. In our program, we keep this in check by consistently reinforcing the following premise to young players, **"Remember guys, these games are for learning and improving your skills. If we win it is a bonus, but winning is not the main objective today."**

As Professor Frank Smoll and his colleagues affirm, **"Well-informed coaches realize that success is not equivalent to winning games."**[24] Leading youth soccer coaches working within the academies of top European clubs **use games primarily for learning**; they do not utilize games in the conventional fashion so often witnessed throughout youth soccer in the U.S. Rather than adopting a short-term perspective and teaching their young players that 'success' resides in winning, these elite coaches focus on the long-term development of their players and understand that they must create a positive learning environment that focuses on skill improvement and game understanding. As Professor Joe Baker and his colleagues point out, "The ability of the coach to devise an environment that **fosters optimal learning** becomes one of the most significant keys to athlete development."[25]

In order to exemplify this, researchers Dr. C. Cushion and M. Smith undertook a study investigating the in-game behaviors of top level youth soccer coaches in the U.K. who are responsible for the development of the country's best talent. They determine how youth coaches employed by some of England's major professional soccer clubs clearly utilize games primarily as a learning platform. Winning is not the priority for these elite coaches, and in reference to one particular coach and his club, Smith and Cushion note, "Despite the elite nature of the program, winning was de-emphasized; no scores or league positions were kept. The focus was on improving and developing individual players rather than the team's win/loss record."[26]

Additionally, two other coaches interviewed in this particular study concisely expressed their approach towards games during the early stages of development:

Coach A: "I say, look I don't mind what the score is at the end of the game. Try things in the game which we were practicing during the week."

Coach B: "It's an open doorway to learning. It's providing the players with the best opportunity to achieve their goal, whatever that goal is."

Research by Dr. Nicholas Holt of the University of Alberta, discussing soccer talent development systems in various countries accentuated how this approach is taken by elite coaches all over the globe.[27] In his study, a leading coach working with players between 15-18 years of age discussed the need for players to be acquainted with various systems of play. He affirmed that it was his job as a coach to teach them different formations, such as 4-4-2, 4-5-1, and 3-5-2, and the positional responsibilities of each formation **(in 4-4-2 the coach is employing four defenders, four midfielders and two forwards)**. He was also aware that playing the same formation every week would most likely increase the chances of winning as players would become more accustomed to their roles because they would be constantly repeating the same patterns of play and getting into the same defensive units. This coach understood that changing formations was likely to unsettle his team and therefore decrease their chances of winning because players would face more problems and make more mistakes. Nonetheless, he understood his main objective as a youth coach, and how the players' **understanding of different systems and formations was essential to their individual development and certainly more important than producing game wins at that moment**.

Again, taking this path is difficult if the coach cannot detach his ego or is under pressure to produce wins. The example from Holt's study is demonstrated clearly in the following scenario:

Coach 'A' has been working on the 4-4-2 formation with his players for the last month. During that time they have become very efficient with it and have performed really well, winning the last few games comfortably. However, the coach begins working with the players on the 3-5-2 system, and in their next game, due to finding it difficult playing with only 3 designated defenders and being unfamiliar with the different positional responsibilities, they find themselves 3 - 0 down at half time.

*At this point the coach knows if he goes back to his 4-4-2 system his team could get back into the game and may even be able to win it. He also has other coaches and parents watching the game who are probably thinking, "This coach hasn't got his team playing well together at all!" But he does not let his ego get in the way, and he **stays true to the objective** of developing his players' understanding of the 3-5-2 system.*

*So at half time **Coach 'A'** points out the problems, asks them a few questions, and collectively they develop their understanding on how to fix those problems. They go out in the second half and looking much more organized end up losing the game 3 - 1. The coach brings them in after the game and explains how happy he is with their performance and their ability to improve by solving the problems they discussed at half time. For the next few weeks they continue to work on the 3-5-2 formation and their knowledge and understanding of that system improves greatly.*

A significant point we must highlight from this study is that we see a coach who is working with players between the ages of 15-18; but even with these older age groups, leading youth soccer coaches are taking a **developmental approach** toward games and not placing the main emphasis on winning. Taking such an outlook with players of this age really augments the need for coaches who are working with younger players to utilize games primarily as a learning tool in the development process.

It is useful to offer the thoughts of former elite coach Juan Santisteban who coached the Spanish National youth teams at various age groups and helped nurture the current Barcelona stars Xavi and Iniesta. In relation to winning, Santisteban further exposes the misguided actions of those organizations passionately placing trophy hunting and winning as their top priorities by saying, **"As usual, I was less concerned with results than with adding to the boys' education."**[28]

In response to this philosophy, UEFA Technical Director Andy Roxburgh in his article 'The Da Vinci Coach' says:

> Of course, coaches and players want to win, **but not at the expense of the young players' health and development**. The players' welfare and enjoyment supersedes team outcomes – in fact, the win-at-all-cost mentality has no place in the grassroots game or, for that matter, in elite youth football [soccer].[29]

This perspective was echoed in the numerous discussions that we had with elite coaches during our research. For example, in December, 2009, John Allpress, the National Player Development Manager with the English Football Association (The FA), offered us insights through his experiences working in youth development. As a coach working with the England U16 Boys soccer team, John helped cultivate players such as Wayne Rooney, Theo Walcott and James Milner, all of whom who have progressed to the elite standards of the game playing in the English Premier League (EPL) and representing their country at the highest level. Allpress told us how he and the rest of the coaching staff approached games with the English team:

> **Games are all about helping players improve.** For example, we would focus our half time reviews on the learning objectives we set before the game, rather than the score. Therefore, we could be losing, but if we witnessed the players trying the things we spoke about before the game, we would praise them. On the other hand, we could be winning, but if players were not attempting things we had referred to before the game we would remind them that the main goal was learning.

In 2010, at the Carrington training ground Dean Whitehouse, a youth soccer coach working in the academy at Manchester United Football Club in England, also offered us a number of important views on the issue of youth development in soccer. The striking feature of our discussion was his perspective on how the youth academy at Manchester United utilized games:

> It is crucial that everyone understands that games should be utilized for learning and players feel they have the freedom to express themselves. **We realize that the final score is not as important as learning at this moment.** If young players are pressured to win every time they step on the field, they will not receive the opportunities that are vital to their development, nor will they feel confident about practicing and implementing new skills or ideas.

Undoubtedly, the way elite coaches utilize games severely contrasts with the conventional approach taken by so many clubs and coaches in U.S. youth soccer. Helping players maintain a strong desire to continue their involvement in the sport and allowing them the opportunity to unlock their potential means that we must primarily utilize games from a learning perspective. What many coaches and parents must appreciate is that most people quickly forget about today's score. But young players **will always remember** those adults who offered positive support, guidance, and freedom to express their capabilities.

Coaching Outside the Box: Changing the Mindset in Youth Soccer

Chapter Two

Sideline Instruction

"We all have a built-in, natural learning capability that is actually disrupted by instruction".[30]

Sir John Whitmore - Sports Psychologist and Performance Coach

Although providing clear instruction and guidance at appropriate moments can facilitate young players' learning, many coaches and parents make the mistake of relentlessly bombarding youngsters with information and directions during games. These coaches and parents habitually bellow instructions and completely overload players **(many of whom are novices struggling to execute fundamental skills and techniques)** with excessive information without considering the ramifications of this behavior on the youth's overall development and immediate experiences.

Many coaches and parents fail to understand that when they take this approach they end up creating a chaotic commotion that serves no help to anyone and simply suppresses the players' liberty to make their own decisions. For example, some of the most popular phrases and instructions that can be heard from the sideline robotically yelled are:

- *"Pass it!"*
- *"Shoot!"*
- *"Clear it!"*
- *"Be Aggressive!"*
- *"Go, Go, Go!"*
- *"Not in the middle!"*

Furthermore, not only do many coaches and parents constantly relay such instructions, but due to their overzealous nature many attempt to pass on multiple points at once. When they take this approach, coaches and parents unwittingly end up overloading young players with 3 or 4 different coaching points often leaving them completely **confused** and with no real focus on any particular objective.

Here is a simple example of how coaches overload a player with numerous instructions at once:

> *Alex, you've got to pass the ball as soon as they're wide open and then overlap, but if we lose the ball get back quick on defense and mark your player!*

But regardless of whether coaches or parents are overloading players with multiple instructions or directing them with single word commands, **why do so many feel as though it is their responsibility to constantly tell players what to do and create a scenario where young players are machines who are there to merely execute their instructions?**

First of all, many coaches and parents do not even think about why they are doing it. They witness others constantly offering instruction in youth soccer, at various youth sport events, or at college and professional levels, so they simply repeat it without question and it becomes a habit.

Many coaches and parents have benevolent motives, and believe they are helping their players by constantly imparting advice and instructions from the sidelines. There are also those who unwittingly assume it is their role to constantly tell players what to do and how to do it, convinced that if they do not perform this duty then they are not effective as coaches or displaying good parental support.

Many **coaches also allow their egos to influence their sideline behavior** and become preoccupied with exhibiting an air of control, authority, and expertise, feeling they must behave in a way that befits what they consider the archetypical coach by pointing to, directing, and constantly shouting instructions to their players. More concerned about their coaching ego than about their players' best interests, these coaches strive to be seen as commanding figures and constantly consider how parents and administrators may be evaluating them.

In their study investigating practice and skill acquisition in soccer, researchers Professor Mark Williams and Dr. Nicola Hodges reaffirm this point: "Unfortunately, some coaches feel the need to justify their existence and consider that this is best achieved through a vociferous, authoritarian style [of coaching]".[31]

But it is important to note that many parents and administrators often **demand and expect** that their coach be highly vocal and commanding from the sidelines. This they believe constitutes good coaching practice. So, as long as the coach is pointing at, directing, and telling players what to do at every turn, a high percentage of parents and administrators feel satisfied. This is another reason why many coaches (especially those who are paid money for their coaching services) play the role of the 'sideline general'!

Many parents constantly direct their child from the sidelines **because they are desperate for their child to play well** due to the personal fulfillment they receive. Conversely, if their child's performance level is not reaching their desired standard, this frequently results in them feeling depressed, dismayed, and frustrated. So, more concerned with their own feelings of self-worth as a result of their child looking good on the field parents relentlessly shout instructions as they believe it increases the chances of this outcome. According to sports psychologists, this overreliance on the child's performance influencing the parents' gratification and dejection is what is referred to as the '**reverse dependency trap**', which can be very destructive for their child's early experiences and future in the sport.[32]

However, the primary driver as to why so many coaches and parents constantly tell young players what to do on the soccer field is because of the win-at-all-cost mentality. Many believe that their commands and directions increase their team's chances of winning.

Evidence suggesting that this is the case is how the ceaseless instruction and direction is frequently at its peak when the score line is close. But this diminishes considerably when the possibility of winning is seemingly out of reach. During our research, we encountered numerous occasions where coaches and parents were vociferous and instructive, but when their team went 3 or 4 goals down they barely said a word, having 'thrown in the towel' and given up pursuing the desired result. So again, what happened to the notion that *"The most important thing is that the children are having fun - **it's not that important if they win or lose."?*** If these coaches and parents truly adhered to this philosophy, their emotions and interest in the game would not deviate in such a dramatic fashion.

We only have to take a look at the popular shout of **"Not in the middle"** to affirm this. Coaches and parents commonly scream this command when their players play the ball in the middle of the field close to their own goal, reacting this way due to the fear that one of their players will make a mistake and present an easy scoring opportunity to the opposition, even though playing in these areas is an excellent way for young players to learn and develop their understanding of the game.

Finally, further evidence to suggest that instruction from the sideline is primarily for winning purposes is how many coaches constantly command their players to pass the ball to their most effective or skillful member of the team. Often, this player is more likely to score goals or cause trouble for the opposition. But the fact that other players are often bypassed due to this tactic and have to squander opportunities important to their own developmental needs is frequently overlooked by many.

It is important that coaches, parents, and administrators understand the detrimental impact consistent sideline intervention has on players' long-term development and immediate experiences. Horst Wein, an elite youth soccer coach who has worked with some of the major professional academies in Europe, states "Coaches are used to giving away their knowledge through many instructions without being aware that **coaching this way will limit their players' development**".[33]

With its unpredictable, frenetic, and uncertain nature, soccer presents various situations for players to make split second decisions and work out problems by implementing inventive techniques, skills, or ideas. So coaches and parents persistently barking instructions from the sidelines **simply stifle the players' ability to learn** and to develop their creativity because the opportunity to take ownership of the decision making process is taken away during such critical moments.

Young players not given the chance to make their own decisions or the opportunity to allow their individual flair and imagination to flourish often lack imagination and become rigid and predictable in the long-term. In their study investigating the perspectives of elite coaches on effective talent development, Dr. Martindale and his colleagues offer the following viewpoint of a leading coach, *"Players who are directed all the time lack self-awareness and become robotic"*.[34]

Constant instruction and direction from the sideline is a common theme in U.S. youth soccer that negatively impacts young players' experiences and development.

The following scenario demonstrates how persistent intervention suppresses the chance for players to develop their inventiveness, problem solving, and decision making capabilities:

*Jimmy is dribbling the ball up the field and getting close to goal when an opposing player approaches to tackle him. Jimmy's teammate Billy is wide open on the left side of the field. The coach starts to scream to Jimmy, **"Pass to Billy!!! Quick, pass to Billy!!!"** Jimmy, hearing the coach, immediately passes the ball out wide to Billy, who strikes the ball past the goalkeeper to score.*

In this particular circumstance, many coaches and parents will likely assume this to be effective coaching as the directions that Jimmy receives makes it easier for him to make a successful pass and helped his team score. However, telling Jimmy what to do and when to do it, the coach deprives Jimmy of a learning opportunity by making the decision for him and denying him the chance to assess the situation and find a creative solution to the problem for himself.

Additionally, in this scenario the coach also misses an excellent learning opportunity to evaluate Jimmy's progress. By telling Jimmy what to do and when to do it, the coach loses the chance to see what he would have done had he received no instruction from the sideline. But now the coach will never know. Therefore, a good question at this juncture is **how can we evaluate what players have learned and what players are capable of doing, if we constantly tell them what to do and deny them the opportunity to show us what they know?**

A further point using the last example is that we have to consider that Jimmy may have been eager to try to beat the opposing player by experimenting with a new skill, rather than taking the option of passing the ball. The challenge of dribbling past an opponent is a situation many players are faced with and have to execute if they want to advance towards the opponent's goal. **This imaginative trait and ability distinguishes the most successful soccer players.** So undoubtedly this should be encouraged and developed during a young player's early and influential years. John Peacock, the England U17's Boys National Coach, supports this view and advocates an approach that allows players to take ownership of decisions as much as possible:

Too readily we tell our players to pass and obviously through good combination play we can get to the other side of the defense. However, what happens when players are isolated 1 v 1 in attacking areas and they don't possess the necessary qualities to go past anyone? We may have to start playing negatively, i.e. backwards or square, or even worse, lose possession through inefficient skill when facing an opponent.[35]

Again, directing players to pass and telling them when to shoot or clear the ball not only deprives them of the freedom that will help them become more creative and intelligent soccer players, but also inadvertently **restrains players' immediate enjoyment levels**. Ultimately, all coaches and parents must understand that overbearing instruction often results in young players becoming uninspired by the sport.

In their book <u>More than Goals</u>, Mike Woitalla and former captain of the U.S. national soccer team and current U.S. Youth Soccer Technical Director, Claudio Reyna, use an excellent analogy to articulate how this sideline instruction negatively impacts young players' experiences and appetite for the sport:

> For some reason, adults – some who can't even kick a ball – think it's perfectly ok to scream at children while they're playing soccer. How normal would it seem if a mother gave a six year old some crayons and a coloring book and started screaming, "Use the red crayon! Stay in the lines! Don't use yellow!?" **Do you think that child would develop a passion for drawing?**[36]

From our early days as young soccer players right through to the professional level, we conclude that there is nothing more irritating when playing than having someone constantly directing you and telling you what to do. Additionally, while coaching youth soccer, we have observed firsthand many young players becoming despondent, de-motivated, and frustrated due to the conventional approach toward sideline intervention being taken by their coaches and parents.

This state of affairs undoubtedly increases the chances of young players disengaging from the sport. In their investigation of the factors contributing to the drop out in youth sports, researchers Dr. Fraser-Thomas and colleagues substantiate this by claiming, *"An autocratic style of coaching has been associated with negative outcomes such as negative attitudes towards coaches, decreased motivation and dropout"*.[37]

Investigating sideline behavior within youth soccer, researchers Dr. La Voi and Assistant Professor Jens Omli attempted to determine the effects that adult intervention has on young players' development. In their study, **they establish that comments and sideline behaviors are often characterized by frustration and anger** which magnifies further the detrimental impact sideline instruction has on the experiences and well-being of youth soccer players.[38]

This is something we have observed consistently in youth soccer. Often this scenario arises because coaches and parents become frustrated that things are not going well for their team. As many fail to consider factors such as the ability of the opposition, their own players' capabilities, or that young players may be lacking in confidence *(possibly because they are being critiqued with every play)*, these adults automatically assume that players are simply not listening to their instructions. Therefore, they begin to get angry and their sideline direction becomes even louder and begins to take on an aggressive form.

So not only are coaches and parents bombarding young players with overwhelming amounts of instruction which is detrimental to the players' learning and enjoyment, but the negative consequences are intensified further due to many **young players feeling intimidated** from such sideline rage. By hijacking youth soccer games in this inappropriate fashion, how do we expect young players to enjoy their experiences and develop effectively?

Based on the evidence presented so far in this chapter, it is truly remarkable that so many self-proclaimed leading clubs in the U.S. (who charge significant fees for their services) claiming that player development is their main focus not only employ coaches who constantly direct young players from the sidelines, but also allow parents to relentlessly overload players with instructions and commands. Time and time again, we have observed how parents at these clubs gather on the sidelines as though it is both their responsibility and right to tell young players what to do. Why are these clubs claiming to have the primary objective of player development allowing this to happen, considering the **detrimental effect this has on the players' development and immediate experiences?**

In many cases, it is because administrators and coaches are fearful of upsetting parents by informing them they **cannot** tell players (including their own children) what to do on the field. Of course, many clubs claim to have this kind of rule in place, but if you go and watch one of their games the parents' actions clearly demonstrate that it is simply not being enforced. But this is another façade of acceptance. These clubs would not dare tell parents that if they fail to abide by this rule they must leave their organization. Therefore, more concerned with the danger of parents becoming dissatisfied and taking their child to another club than the **true development** of their players, these administrators and coaches choose to say **nothing**.

For many self-proclaimed 'premier' clubs, this path is the one to take, as it often reduces the risk of players leaving and maintains higher numbers in the organization, which in turn increases revenue: **Another classic case of business before development.** Additionally, losing a 'star player' due to enforcing rules and upsetting parents has the potential of reducing their chances of short-term success and trophy accumulation, which ultimately damages the winning reputation they so desperately pursue.

Increasing imagination, creativity, and learning opportunities

Throughout the years we have always appreciated how the players' decision making skills, imagination, and creativity on the field are pivotal factors in their becoming effective soccer players. Again, the world's greatest players have reached that status because they are exceptional in these key areas.

It is no surprise that studies indicate decision making skills, imagination, and the players' overall awareness on the field are the strongest indicators that young players will progress in the game to the professional status. In their study investigating the key factors for talent development in soccer, researchers Dr. Rianne Kannekens and colleagues point out how young players who demonstrate superior decision-making skills are the players that reach higher levels of the game when they become adults. They also stress how it is extremely difficult for players to be successful in the future if they do not develop this crucial aspect of the game during the formative years of involvement in the sport.[39]

Therefore, it is essential that coaches and parents allow young players the freedom to make their own decisions on the playing field and refrain from instructing them through each phase of play. In The Talent Code, Daniel Coyle substantiates this perspective using the thoughts of leading sports coach Robert Lansdorp, **"If it's a choice between me telling them to do it, or them figuring it out, I'll take the second option every time. You've got to make the kid an independent thinker, a problem-solver. The point is they have got to figure things out for themselves."**[40]

In our program, we have constantly encouraged all coaches and parents to embrace this perception in order to facilitate players in their overall development and enhance their enjoyment, motivation, and confidence levels. Our message is to allow players to get on with things under the coaches' **guidance and support** rather than under the coaches' and parents' overbearing **command**. Essentially, our objective is to change the mindset from one that views the coach as a 'sideline general' to one that views the coach as a facilitator of learning.

Well informed coaches recognize that they don't need to be constantly directing and shouting from the sidelines. Sitting and observing in a relaxed manner is a far more effective approach.

But for many parents new and unfamiliar to this approach, it often causes curiosity, leading them to ask why the coaches are so quiet, and why they are not more vocal and controlling on the sidelines. However, after they have been informed that this approach is a deliberate strategy to facilitate their child's overall development, it relieves their initial concerns and often causes healthy inquisitiveness.

This supportive approach is advocated by a number of top-level youth coaches who acknowledge that young players should be viewed as active problem solvers and provided with the responsibility for their own actions on the field. Investigating the game-day behaviors of leading youth soccer coaches at professional academies in England, researchers Dr. C. Cushion and M. Smith state:

Silence was considered necessary by the coaches to observe and analyze, and was used as a method to encourage the players to learn for themselves. Without intervention from the coach, it was believed that the players could encourage their own sensory feedback. Consequently, **silence was used as a tool for learning. The coaches expressed concern that too much intervention would deny the players not only the opportunities to learn but also the opportunity to demonstrate what has already been learnt.**[41]

In addition, three elite coaches in this study offered the following thoughts on intervention from the sidelines:

Coach A: "I want them to be unencumbered by the pressure of my voice. So I want to let them go through the processes of making decisions and choices during the course of the game unfettered by me telling them what to do and when to do it".

Coach B: "Your automatic instinct is to help the kids and you think helping the kids is actually giving instruction. When it might be more helpful if you don't, if you let the kids make their own mistakes. That would be a better way for learning".

Coach C: "I want the players to learn for themselves. **I don't want prescribed motions of play.** The kids have got to learn, find out through their own learning experiences".

This perspective is reinforced by former international soccer player Trevor Brooking the Technical Director for the English Football Association responsible for the progress of England's youth players and national game. Discussing his views on the development of young players, he used a shining example afforded by the coaches working at the academy of Manchester United FC: "*The Manchester United philosophy is to let them discover it themselves. The old vision of the coach shouting do this or do that has gone. What they have realized at United is the best coaching for youngsters is about standing back*".[42]

Note: This was something we observed first hand during our visits to Manchester United's training facilities when we watched the academy train and play.

Looking at some of the most successful players in the history of the game, we see many spent countless hours playing in environments **with no adult intervention** and organized structure. Playing soccer on the streets, in local parks, or in any free space, allowed them freedom and enhanced their learning possibilities through experimenting, taking risks, making their own decisions, and pure enjoyment. Arguably the greatest player of the modern era, Argentinean and Barcelona superstar Lionel Messi relates his current philosophy of playing to the unconstrained manner that allowed him to develop his fantastic talents as a young boy, "I play like a child. I think about myself on a small field, or in the street, I see myself with the ball in the same way as I am now. I have not changed at all. You must remember soccer is a game to have fun and you play for that".[43]

Dutch legend Johan Cruyff, an exponent of the <u>Total Football</u> philosophy exhibited by the famous Holland international teams of the 1970's, also affords insightful views on how young players should be permitted the freedom to play **without** constant adult intervention maintaining that:

> Children should do nothing but play and play. **Children should play with total freedom and enjoyment without any pressure or any shouting from the coach that can turn every game into a case of life or death.** My generation learned to play soccer on the street. Our skill levels greatly improved because **we** were always involved in the game. The street was our soccer school.[44]

These perspectives are further reaffirmed in research by Dr. Salmela and Dr. Moreas who investigated the history of 22 Brazilian youth soccer players aged 16-18 selected for professional soccer clubs. In their study, they established that until they were selected by clubs in their later teens, these players had **received little or no structured coaching**.[45] Once again the driving principle we can take from this evidence is that playing in a free and positive environment that allows players to make their own decisions and be accountable for them is essential for their development.

We must make an imperative point at this stage. When working with young players, we do not advocate that coaches should be silent and uninvolved throughout the entirety of the game. It is important to understand that there are key moments when coaches can facilitate the players' self-learning by using **subtle cues and timely advice**. We will now touch on a few examples of how offering short phrases, questions, and constructive feedback can assist the young players' learning and understanding.

- **'What do you see?'** – *This question encourages a player in possession of the ball to get their head up and assess their options.*

- **'Scan'** – *This helps to develop the players' awareness of what is around them on the field when they are not in possession of and/or are about to receive the ball.*

- **'Relax'** – *This cue, delivered in a calm tone, develops the players' composure on the field and encourages them to think about their choices. It is particularly useful for novice players who may be nervous or lacking in technical proficiency.*

- **'What can you try?'** – *This question motivates players to attempt new skills and be creative. It also helps to reaffirm the message that the game is a learning platform.*

- **'How can you help?'** – *This encourages players to support the player on the ball, help teammates defend, and create further attacking options in the final third.*

Additionally, choosing appropriate moments to offer positive support and guidance can have a very powerful effect. For example, briefly speaking individually to a player in a relaxed manner at half-time or after they have had a drink will often have much more impact than trying to explain your thoughts while they are engaged in play. Additionally, if a player attempts a skill or does something well on the field, announcing in front of everyone that their effort was excellent is a great way to boost their confidence while affirming to other players and parents that you are striving to create a positive learning environment. Furthermore, in their book <u>Communication Basics,</u> authors Judy Jennings and Linda Malcak demonstrate that "The single most powerful form of communication is non-verbal. More than 80% of communication occurs without words, hence the expression 'actions speak louder than words'".[46] Therefore, using some positive body language such as a smile or thumbs up to compliment players can be very effective.

Actions can speak louder than words and can have a positive impact when delivered at the appropriate moment.

Finally, since the aim of this chapter is to demonstrate philosophically how the approach, in terms of instruction from the sideline, needs to be altered from the conventional one which bombards players with instruction to one that offers players an appropriate amount of freedom, we are merely touching the surface on what methods you can implement from a positive coaching standpoint. An important point when utilizing these methods to guide players is that you only **use them occasionally**. Additionally, it is essential that coaches do not overuse the same methods when offering positive reinforcement, such as robotically yelling **"good job"** or **"way to go"** consistently throughout the game. When coaches make these mistakes it is often counterproductive and diminishes the power and effect of your message as players become aware that this praise is being offered way too generously and it is not from the heart.

We must reiterate, our experiences and the evidence we have looked at suggests that young players must be provided with **sustained periods of freedom, silence, and uninterrupted play** throughout the early stages of their development in order to enhance their creativity, ability to make astute decisions, and solve problems. Providing young players with this autonomy will always increase their enjoyment, confidence, and chances of developing a passion for the game and exploring their potential.

Chapter Three

Dealing with Mistakes

"If we have to deprive a player of the right to make mistakes, then we'd best hang up everything and go home".[47]

Giovanni Trapatonni - The most successful coach in professional Italian soccer

It should be expected that players **(many of whom are novices struggling to execute fundamental skills and techniques)** in their formative years will often make mistakes. How coaches and parents deal with this during the early stages of the players' development is an essential issue in youth soccer. For many years we have witnessed coaches and parents react in an unacceptable manner when young players make a mistake on the field. These actions range from inappropriate to disgraceful, harmful, and even abusive behavior.

But the way mistakes are dealt with negatively could be attributed to various reasons. For example, some coaches and parents believe that regularly shouting at or criticizing young players when they make a mistake is an effective method of coaching which motivates players to perform at a higher level. Once again, many coaches allow their ego to get in the way and feel as though their players' mistakes reflect negatively on their coaching ability. Likewise, parents frequently get caught in the **'reverse dependency trap'** and allow their child's mistakes to influence their emotional state of mind. However, there can be no doubt that the major reason why many coaches and parents deal with mistakes inappropriately is because of the **win-at-all-cost mentality**.

But regardless of the reasons why mistakes are dealt with inappropriately, we must appreciate how it negatively impacts young players' immediate experiences and development in the sport. To help our understanding, we will look at some notable scenarios indicative of our observations throughout the U.S.

Scenario 1:

*One evening we observed a U9 soccer game. A coach, **who was being paid by parents for training their children**, was becoming especially animated, angry, and frustrated throughout the game, exemplified by his negative body language and his inappropriate comments directed at the referee and at his own players when they conceded a goal. The decisive moment came towards the end of the game when one of his players was attacking the outside with the ball. With a teammate wide open in the goal-box the coach shouted at the player in possession to pass. Instead, the player took a shot and unfortunately dragged it wide of the goal. Clearly annoyed, the coach immediately substituted the player. He then continued to scold the youth on the sidelines by yelling, **"Why didn't you pass?!?!?" "You cannot miss a chance like that!!! What are doing?!?!?** The young player (age 8 or 9) stood beside the coach, rubbing his hands nervously, looking down at the ground.*

Scenario 2:

*Only a few minutes into a U11 game we observed a coach, who worked for a 'self-proclaimed' leading club, directing his anger and frustration at one of his players. When two youngsters came together to tackle for the ball and his player failed to win the challenge, the coach immediately jumped up off the bench and screamed, **"If you're going to tackle like a six year old, you can sit next to me. In fact, come and sit next to me on the bench!"** Visibly dejected, the young player made his way over to the bench and sat with his head down.*

In both examples, the coaches displayed neither discretion nor compassion whatsoever and screamed at young players in front of their teammates, parents, and other spectators. Furthermore, these coaches reacted in a common fashion by substituting their players immediately after they had made a mistake. But as winning is the main objective for these coaches this is a natural step as the danger of the player making the same mistake is minimized. We question why these coaches feel that shouting negative comments and taking these actions with young players is appropriate. Don't they care about the development of these children, **or is this happening because they are preoccupied with what these children are or aren't doing for them?** How can we expect young players to enjoy their experiences and the sport if this is happening?

To put this in context, imagine your child coming home from school to inform you that he or she had been screamed at, ridiculed, and sent out of the classroom by the teacher in front of the other pupils **for simply making a mistake on a math quiz**. Many parents would feel a sense of outrage with such a situation. The notion that in the classroom a schoolteacher has become frustrated and angry with your child for simply making a mistake and then displayed their irritation through scolding or critical comments is unacceptable. However, exactly this situation unfolds time after time on soccer fields all over the nation, while parents and youth soccer administrators simply accept this behavior as the norm and do not expect anything better.

What are you doing?!?!? - Adults dealing with young players' mistakes in a negative and harsh manner is a common theme in U.S. youth soccer

As in Scenarios 1 and 2, many coaches and parents have no problem revealing their frustrations and anger vociferously for all to hear. But some try concealing their emotions and deliver their disapproval in other ways. The following scenario demonstrates this point:

Scenario 3:

*We had a parent in our program whose 8 year old son made a mistake during a game that resulted in a goal for the opposing team. The young player was **rightly** trying an imaginative piece of skill, but it went wrong and the ball ended up in his own goal. Although at first he was comfortable with this mistake (as we immediately reassured him that everything was fine and that we were in fact happy he was trying to be creative), he made eye contact with his father who gave him a cold stare that the young child clearly knew too well. This player instantly got upset; so we brought him over to the sideline and calmed him down.*

Although this parent wasn't shouting or conveying his frustration openly, this discreet approach still had a detrimental impact on the young player, the ramifications of which we will discuss shortly. After this incident, we privately informed the player's father that he must remember that his child is being encouraged to be creative and try things **without fear of failure**. Therefore, if his child makes a mistake, we need to let him know that it is perfectly acceptable. We never want parents or our coaches behaving in a manner where players feel bad for making mistakes.

Coaches and parents repeatedly exhibit negative body language as a way to express and communicate disapproval when a mistake has been made. And looking at the 'cold stare' in scenario 3 allows us to realize how potent this form of communication can be. But whether coaches and parents shake their heads, roll their eyes, throw their arms out, or look up at the sky, it immediately lets players know that what they have just done is unacceptable.

Another common form of expressing frustration is the use of sarcasm. For example, the sarcastic question of **"Who's that to?"** directed at a player who has just accidentally passed the ball to the opposing team is a very frequent response from coaches and parents. Often this question is delivered with resentment or occasionally with fake laughter to mask the coaches' and parents' true emotions. Rarely is this question followed by constructive feedback, its only purpose being for coaches and parents to vent their irritation due to being annoyed at the player who made the mistake. Furthermore, this is regularly aimed at young players who fail to understand the sarcasm anyway!

Regardless of whether coaches and parents are expressing their annoyance openly or using subtle methods to vent their frustration, we must ask the following questions, when young players are trying to learn and enjoy the sport, does the behavior we have previously outlined constitute rational support? Quite clearly it does not; **screaming, ridiculing, or punishing young children for making a mistake is irrational.** What are these coaches and parents thinking? Or are they not thinking at all due to being so immersed in the **outcome** of the game?

Maybe if these coaches and parents had a better understanding of how their actions and behavior negatively impacts young players' immediate experiences and development they would stop.

A significant amount of research helps us comprehend how detrimental it can be when dealing with mistakes in this manner. For example, in their study investigating emotional abuse on young players by adults, psychologist Dr. Misia Gervis and Nicola Dunn of Brunel University in England labeled humiliating, belittling, shouting, or threatening by adults **as emotional abuse.** The players interviewed for this study commented on how after being subjected to negative comments they felt **stupid, worthless, depressed, humiliated, hurt, fearful, angry, and lacking in self-confidence.**[48]

We can expect that young soccer players will experience these feelings when scolded or humiliated by a coach or parent more motivated by 'winning' or their child performing well rather than by the welfare and development of young players. In the short-term, there are also further detrimental implications from this type of behavior which many coaches and parents fail to recognize. For example, many players will emulate this type of derogatory behavior, aiming it towards their own teammates and the officials, which over time will breed a culture where scolding, negative, and abusive comments become an accepted part of the youth soccer environment and of **their lives off the field.**

A critical point all coaches and parents need to understand is that when the environment is hostile and intimidating and players fear making a mistake, **they get on edge and are more likely to make further mistakes**. This unfortunately perpetuates a negative cycle of poor coaching behavior which denies young players needed physical and emotional development. Researchers Gervis and Dunn substantiate this point:

> These feelings are indicative of a **destructive cycle** in which the athlete exhibits a lack of belief in their own ability to perform. This is often referred to as low performance self-efficacy, which culminates in performance detriments. Those in turn, **intensify the abusive behavior of adults**, as performance expectations are not met.[49]

But during this destructive cycle, many parents, coaches, and administrators simply assume that a young player is underperforming due to other factors. For example, they may feel that the player is failing to apply the necessary levels of effort or simply lacking ability. However, young players caught in this cycle are more likely to underperform due to their lack of self-confidence or because they are **wracked with fear**.

Many players who realize they will be persistently scolded every time they make a mistake will try to hide on the field and display a diminished appetite to receive the ball. Furthermore, players will often look towards the sidelines after making an error to assess the magnitude of their mistake through the reaction of their coach or parent. Scenario 3 demonstrates this point. Here a child intuitively knew that his father would be unhappy (hence why he looked over at him) and that he would have to face the consequences for **accidently** putting the ball in his own goal.

Working with many families and young players over the years, it became evident that many parents fail to recognize how powerful and detrimental their words, actions, and evaluations of their own children can be. Many times we have seen a player in the early stages of their development make mistakes in a practice or game and afterwards observe their parent's eagerness to take it into their own hands by criticizing the young player's mistakes as soon as they reach the parking lot. Frequently, the child clearly does not want to engage in the discussion, and most likely just wants to get in the car and enjoy the rest of the day. Again, many of these parents will proclaim that their child's enjoyment is a major concern. But how can they expect their child's enjoyment to be enhanced if the child is demonstrating resistance to their critical feedback? Our experiences with this situation demonstrate that young players consistently subjected to this overbearing behavior tend to exhibit less confidence and interest in the sport. Therefore, we always recommend that parents leave it to us as coaches to deal with their child's faults or mistakes, and refrain from attempting to provide them with their own opinions, especially if their child expresses reluctance to take it on board.

Again, the major objective of any coach or parent during the early stages of the players' development should be to provide them with a positive and enjoyable environment that cultivates an enduring passion for the game. Therefore, constantly highlighting young players' mistakes and berating their play will not be a forward step toward this goal and will more likely lead to negative repercussions in the long-term. Paul Bickerton, sport scientist and former coach development mentor at Sports Coach UK, emphasizes this point: "The attitudes to sporting ability are our greatest challenge today. Young people have been turned away from sport, not as a result of choice, but of **perceived failure or incompetence**."[50]

Dealing with mistakes positively

When dealing with mistakes during the early stages of development, it is essential for coaches to maintain a positive and realistic outlook, **one which**

takes the child's emotional and psychological needs into account. While working with many young players of various skill levels and experience, we continuously encourage a philosophy that deals with mistakes positively and constructively while constantly reinforcing the message that mistakes and recognizing them are **essential to the learning process.** This approach allows players to expand their learning capabilities because they can experiment, take risks, and attempt creative skills and ideas without fear.

But when encouraging players to be inventive, we have to be aware that things can break down and players will make mistakes in the process. As Guy Claxton, a Professor in Learning Sciences at the University of Winchester in England proclaims, **"Learning is what we do when we don't know what to do, and if we don't know what to do, sometimes we'll get it wrong and mistakes will happen."**[51] To increase the young players' understanding of the game, self-confidence, creativity, and passion, coaches and parents must embrace this vital perception and deal with mistakes in a fashion that is conducive to the players' development.

To exemplify this point, researchers Dr. C. Cushion and M. Smith document the approaches of elite youth soccer coaches toward mistakes:

Coach A: "Kids should be left to play and make their mistakes; learning comes from mistakes, thinking about it and working out their own answers."

Coach B: "If the kid's playing bad he knows he's having a poor performance. He doesn't need me there to reinforce it in front of everyone. Scolding for me is a thing of the past. They don't need the criticism."

Coach C: "Players that I work with respond well to being told that they're doing a good job. So I try to encourage them and it's fostering a positive environment so that they're not scared of trying things or doing things. So they don't have fear of failure."[52]

These perspectives were reinforced at our visit to the Carrington training ground at Manchester United where we observed training sessions and games for players aged 11-16. In this environment, players were given the freedom to experiment, and if a player did make a mistake, the coaches treated the player positively with support and encouragement. Dean Whitehouse, an academy coach working with Manchester United told us:

> This game, like many others, hinges significantly on confidence. Therefore, we always offer positive, constructive feedback when players make a mistake. Taking this approach ensures that young players remain confident when things don't work out and allows them to develop further understanding of the game. This approach has been hugely productive for so many players over the years, and we wouldn't have it any other way.

Positive body language is another powerful tool a coach can use in motivating and supporting players while guiding them through mistakes. As we mentioned earlier, when players make a mistake, it can be quite common for them to look at their coach or parent. Therefore, at crucial moments positive body language can be very effective, and using a friendly hand gesture or facial expression to signal that all is ok can have a very positive effect when players makes mistakes. Using the following scenario, let us look at two separate responses where the approach is different. Coach A represents the conventional approach discussed earlier, while Coach B represents a positive approach based on learning and development.

Scenario 4:

Just before half time during a U10 soccer game, Michael is in possession of the ball in a defensive area of the field. Under pressure from an opposing player, he attempts to play the ball back to his goalkeeper.

Unfortunately, his pass lacks sufficient power, and the opposing player manages to steal the ball and score before the goalkeeper can get to the ball.

The response of Coach A:

*Coach A immediately throws out his arms and shouts in an aggressive manner for all to hear, "Michael!!! What are you doing?" He then takes Michael out of the game, replaces him with another player, and continues to scold Michael on the touchline. At halftime, he uses Michael's mistake as an example and says to the whole team, "That is exactly why I don't want you guys passing the ball back to the goalkeeper! **If you're back there just clear it!**"*

The response of Coach 'B':

*Coach B waits a few seconds, claps his hands in a positive and motivating manner, and then calls out **"Don't worry guys, it's alright"**. Then at halftime when the opportunity arises, the coach pulls Michael briefly to the side and lets him know that passing the ball back to the goalkeeper was a good decision, but asks him what he could have done differently. Michael explains that he could have passed it harder. The coach agrees and encourages Michael to practice it again the next time the opportunity presents itself.*

The coaches here deal with this mistake quite differently. **Coach A** reacts immediately in a negative manner and without much reflection. He also displays actions that will most likely lead Michael in the future to feeling incompetent, dejected, and fearful of making a mistake, especially as he highlighted Michael's error in front of everyone. This coach also seems upset that his team gave up a goal and says that passing back to the goalkeeper is a risk he does not want them to take. This emphasizes to his players that his primary interest is in the final score and not on his players developing the essential skill of passing back to the goalkeeper.

Immediately, we can observe that **Coach B** is comfortable with his players making mistakes. His actions are positive and supportive, and he addresses the situation in a constructive manner. For example, even though Michael's mistake resulted in giving up a goal, the coach still asked him to attempt passing back to the goalkeeper. This indicates Coach B is primarily concerned that his players learn and try things, **irrespective of the score of the game**. Players in this environment are more likely to feel confident, motivated, and proficient while gaining further knowledge through each experience, positive or negative, that they encounter.

How Coach B confronts this mistake leads us into the final point of this chapter. **Players must confront their mistakes to learn from them.** As John Allpress, the FA National Player Development Manager maintains, "As a coach you help the players best by encouraging them to face their mistakes head on. Players cannot learn anything in denial".[53]

Of course, many players often know when they have made a mistake, especially a technical one, and for that reason, it is not always necessary for the coach to point it out. However, it is crucial for coaches to make sure that players are aware of what has gone wrong and how to confront such a situation constructively in order to maximize the learning opportunity. In our experience, it is far more beneficial for their understanding and learning when players themselves discover what went wrong. A useful technique we have implemented is a process of carrying out some simple questioning (which usually takes place during a resting period i.e. a drink break or half-time). This encourages players to reflect on mistakes and take advantage of them from a learning perspective. For example, some useful questions that can be used are:

- *What did you see happen?*
- *What do you feel went wrong?*
- *What would you do differently if that situation happened again?*

- **What did you learn from this mistake?**

- **How can you improve?**

Our experiences and the evidence we have looked at in this chapter confirms that young players must be allowed to make mistakes and **learn from them**. Recognizing that mistakes are a pivotal aspect of the development process **is the duty of all coaches and parents** involved in youth soccer. Dealing with mistakes in the negative manner we highlighted earlier and failing to utilize them as powerful learning tools is arguably the **biggest mistake of all**.

Chapter Four

Playing Time and Positions

"All of us do not have equal talent, but all of us should have an equal opportunity to develop our talents."[54]

John F. Kennedy

The various positions youngsters can play on the soccer field present different technical, physical, tactical, and psychological challenges allowing them the chance to develop a range of crucial skills. For example, playing as a forward offers young players increased opportunities to practice shooting at the goal and trying to find space in contrast to what a defensive role regularly would. Additionally, defensive roles offer players increased opportunities to work on marking players, blocking shots and facing an opposing forward as the last defender in a one vs. one situation.

Despite this, many coaches conventionally fix or **pigeonhole** players into a specific position week after week throughout the entire season. Repeatedly, coaches will simply proclaim that young players are **'defenders'** or **'forwards'** in spite of the fact they are only eight or nine years old, leaving them tagged with a positional identity throughout their early soccer experiences.

For many involved in youth soccer, this appears to be the intuitive and logical step to take. The rationale for many coaches persistently pigeonholing young players into fixed positions is not based upon player development or what is best for learning. Coaches simply take this path believing that locking players who display specific physical characteristics in set positions week after week increases the chances of **winning**. So again, it appears that these **coaches focus on what players can do for them, rather than on what learning opportunities they, the game, and various positions can offer players.**

For example, young players exhibiting high levels of speed or physical strength (frequently due to being born earlier in the calendar year as we will discuss in more detail in the next chapter) frequently get positioned in a central area of the field because they can utilize these physical attributes to the team's benefit. Obviously, an offensive player who displays superior physical characteristics will have a greater chance of beating opposing defenders and increasing goal scoring opportunities. The same physical attributes may lead coaches to select players for a central defensive position where they can take advantage of their physical prowess to curtail the potential 'threat' from the opposing strikers. But these beneficial attributes should not mean young players get anchored into set positions.

Conversely, there are young players in many youth soccer teams who when compared to others do not exhibit the discernible technical skills or physical characteristics which will afford performance advantages. Due to this, many coaches instantly identify such players as the 'weaker' members of the roster and perceive them as liabilities, and they deliberately attempt to hide the players they perceive as weaker in specific positions so they are not as actively involved in the game. For example, some players will frequently be placed on the left or right side of attack or midfield since the ball will often enter these areas less than it does the central areas of the field. Importantly for these coaches, they recognize that mistakes in wide areas will be less likely to have a major bearing on the score, essentially perceiving these positions as a certain refuge for their 'weaker' players.

Our experiences and observations lead us to conclude that hiding players in such a manner is widespread throughout youth soccer in the U.S. This viewpoint is substantiated by Ian Mulliner, former Director of Coaching for the Illinois Youth Soccer Association, who demonstrates the way this specific issue regularly surfaces at licensed coaching courses in the U.S:

> A common question asked by youth coaches at coaching courses is **'where do I hide my weaker players?'** My answer to that is why do you feel the need to hide them, when it is our job as coaches to develop them. If we never expose those players to situations that arise in games, how do we expect them to get better?[55]

Many coaches fail to recognize the negative consequences that will undoubtedly occur if they consistently restrict players to one position and hide their perceived 'weaker' players during their early years. Although these decisions have the potential to help teams win in the short-term, in the long-term it will certainly hamper many players' overall development and scope for learning.

For example, if young players are consistently placed in a defensive position, the opportunities in which they are encouraged to take a shot on goal or execute an imaginative maneuver in the attacking third of the field will often diminish. Essentially, many young players pigeonholed and labeled as defenders **will have their attacking creativity comprehensively stifled** at a stage of their development when this should be encouraged. Additionally, youngsters who are never allowed to experience the role of playing center midfield *(where often space is limited)* may fail to fully develop their awareness and ability to make quick decisions under pressure from opposing players. Finally, players not acquainted with fundamental defensive responsibilities during their early soccer encounters due to always being utilized as forwards will likely exhibit shortcomings if asked to perform in a defensive or midfield position later in their careers.

This is why locking players in a set position at a young age is strongly opposed by many elite coaches and development experts. For example, U.S. Technical Director Claudio Reyna, who is widely acknowledged as one of the best professional players to be produced in the U.S., reaffirms this perspective on the issue of young players being restricted to one playing position:

> A lot of teams always play their best player in the center of the field. It guarantees he'll get the ball more than anyone else and increase the team's chances of winning. **I played in central midfield, defensive midfield, on the right, on the left, on the wings and in the frontline.** The inclination for our coaches to put their stars in the middle is one reason why our country often has a problem finding talented players to fill the other positions on the field. **And it explains why a lot of young**

stars fade when they hit a higher level. Only accustomed to playing in the middle, they can't adjust to another position, and their careers come to an early end.[56]

A Positive Approach

As we explained in the chapter 'Approach to Games', it is vital that coaches consistently utilize games from a learning perspective that will help players develop critical skills and game understanding. A major aspect of this positive approach is offering players the freedom to play in a **variety of positions** which will enhance their understanding of the game, self-confidence, passion for the sport, and will improve their chance of becoming effective all-round soccer players. In our program, this is why we offer all young players the opportunity to experiment with the various technical, physical, tactical, and psychological demands of each playing position. This can be achieved by moving players into multiple positions during one particular game or by having players experience one position each week and then rotate them into a different position for the next game. The important point being each player samples the various playing positions on a continuous basis throughout their formative years.

We must take note that when players have come to our program from other organizations who pigeonholed them in one position, these players often say *"that's not my position"* or demonstrate resistance to try a different position due to their lacking confidence. Nonetheless, after a little time and encouragement this quickly fades and they embrace the new challenges in a confident manner. Furthermore, these players frequently begin to enjoy the various roles on the field and express that they are learning new integral aspects of the game. Therefore, any coach facing reluctance from a player to attempt another role on the field should always emphasize how important and positive it can be for that player's development and eventually ease them into new experiences.

Exposing young players to a variety of playing positions during the early stages of their development is an approach advocated by many leading coaches working at major professional clubs throughout Europe. In our discussion with Manchester United's Dean Whitehouse, he provided the following thoughts on this topic:

> At Manchester United, our aim with the young kids is to develop their overall understanding of the game from an early age. Therefore, **we ensure that all our players sample different positions**, such as right back [defender], central midfield, or various forward roles. We do not place players into specific positions to increase our chance of winning. That is simply counterproductive for learning and development. We want to allow all players to gain **insight** into the requirements of each position as it helps them to become better all-round players.

This viewpoint is further substantiated by one of the world's best coaches José Mourinho, who has coached at Barcelona, Chelsea, and Real Madrid. He expresses the need for young players to develop the knowledge of a variety of positions: "At this level who knows? A kid that's now playing central defender may in 4 or 5 years be a midfield player. **They don't need to specialize at a young age. They need to go through all the situations.**"[57]

The fact that so many elite coaches emphasize the importance of consistently giving young players the opportunity to experience various playing positions yet again provokes concern regarding the contradictory approach demonstrated by so many self-declared 'leading' youth soccer organizations in the U.S. How can these organizations claim that their primary objective is player development when they consistently anchor young players in specific positions? Either many of these clubs' directors and coaches are misguided, or they are deliberately misleading everyone by keeping players pigeonholed in set positions because winning and trophy accumulation is their true objective. **Providing young players with the opportunity to learn and experience various positions on the field is a must if we are focusing on true player development.**

Minutes on the Field

Our next consideration is the minutes on the field players receive during their early soccer experiences. First, as many parents invest significant and similar amounts of resources in the form of time and money, and in many cases training fees, one would expect from this perspective alone that clubs and coaches should **strive** to offer all young players **equal amounts of playing time**. If coaches want to improve the players' knowledge and understanding of the game and develop their lifelong passion for the sport they must take this approach rather than manipulating this concept to fulfill alternative motives.

Unfortunately, many coaches fail to offer all players equal playing time primarily because winning and team success takes precedence over everyone's individual development. Therefore, the scenario frequently unfolds where **the 'weaker' players on team rosters are banished to prolonged bouts on the sidelines**, enabling the coach to allocate more playing time to the players with more favorable attributes who can produce the win.

In their book <u>Complete Guide to Coaching Education</u>, Professor Daryl Siedentop and colleagues recite a useful anecdote about a young player's experience which helps illustrate this scenario:

> He came to realize that he had a special role on that team. It was neither goalkeeper or full-back, sweeper nor striker; it was the **3-goal player**. That is, when the team was 3 goals ahead, he would get to play, because the game was well in hand. Likewise, if his team was losing 3 to 0, he also got to play, because the coach decided by that stage the team really had no chance to win. Many people tell equivalent sport stories of children spending more time on the sidelines watching and waiting than they do playing. While an increasing focus exists on participation in both youth sport and physical education, a serious commitment to equal opportunity is **seldom present**.[58]

To put this neglectful approach into context, Professor Daniel Frankl of California State University provides an insightful analogy again relating the classroom to the soccer field, **"I cannot even try to imagine a justified scenario in which the teacher and some parents manipulate the system to actively keep some children out of the classroom while allowing other children in."**[59]

It seems that many coaches do not care how their discriminative actions can negatively impact young players. Youngsters who realize that compared to their 'more talented' peers they are only offered minimal playing time will often feel rejected, worthless, incompetent, and ultimately dismayed with their involvement in the sport. Research by Dr. Werner Helsen and his colleagues indicates that many young players consistently subjected to such unequal playing opportunities drop out of the sport altogether at an early age, turning their attention to a sport where they may more readily be selected.[60] Additionally, players limited to minimal or no playing time are deprived of appropriate opportunities to improve their skills and work on various facets of the game. **When this is the case, how can we expect these players to develop and learn?**

When players are subjected to long spells on the bench, how much development is taking place?

But it is not only the so called 'weaker' players that experience negative consequences in relation to the amount of minutes they are granted during games. Those players who are perceived as more talented regularly receive a majority of the playing time, and in some cases consistently play every minute of each game, which can be detrimental to them both in the short and long-term.

First, for those players demonstrating superior ability, the pressure to perform is regularly intensified as coaches frequently place a huge **burden of expectation** on their shoulders to produce game winning performances. After a victory, this message is regularly reinforced as coaches inform the 'more talented' players how significant their performance has been to the team. We have witnessed how this dependability can cause increased levels of stress for the 'more talented' players when the team loses, because their **measurement of success is not based on self-improvement or learning, but is merely based on whether the team won due to the approach and actions taken by the coach.**

Furthermore, as they are constantly allocated the majority of the playing time, these talented players are at significantly higher risk of physical injury. According to Professor Alan Hodson of Leeds Metropolitan University in England and former Head of Sports Medicine at the English Football Association, talented young players are more susceptible to overuse injuries because they are **repeatedly forced to play more minutes on the field than less talented individuals.**[61] As we discuss in more detail in the chapter 'Tournaments', the risk of overuse injuries increases considerably due to clubs', coaches', and parents' incessant drive to win trophies.

Finally, if coaches provide some players with more playing time than others, it repeatedly causes friction and ill-feeling with parents. For example, if their child is not receiving an appropriate amount of playing time, parents often become resentful and angry at the coach. Furthermore, some parents begin to feel bitterness towards other parents whose son or daughter is receiving more playing time in comparison to their own child. These negative aspects undoubtedly increase disharmony and hostility which ultimately hurts the young players.

Fight for Your Place Mentality

When offering preferential treatment by awarding players more playing time due to their performance advantage, coaches naturally promote an ethos whereby players try to prove that they are worthy for a spot on the team. With only a limited number of playing positions, the situation is created where **players try to outdo their teammates** to gain one of the spots in the starting lineup. Unwittingly, many coaches and parents view this scenario as a positive driver, believing it will produce a hard-work mentality and with it better performances from their players to improve the chances of 'glory'.

Even though in many professional team sport settings this concept *(referred to as "competition for places")* is promoted as it often inspires players to constantly work hard and be at the 'top of their game' because otherwise someone else will take their place, we should not thoughtlessly apply the same approach with young children. There is a huge difference that must always be remembered: *Professional players are paid money to perform for the club and the coach, whereas young players are there to enjoy and learn, not fight with their teammates for an opportunity to play!* **This approach has no place during the early stages of the players' development.**

Research strongly suggests that when young players compete for a spot on the team there will be detrimental consequences as it creates an **ego-focused environment**, a destructive setting for players to be involved in. Players consumed with displaying superiority over teammates in order to gain acknowledgement from their coach and ultimately be chosen become far too concerned about how their performance is being evaluated. Professor Craig Stewart and Dr. Michael C. Meyers, investigating motivational traits of young soccer players, reaffirm that this situation fuels a negative environment for young players:

> In an ego focused environment coaches not only emphasize beating the other team, but foster **a rivalry among their own players**, pitting them against each other for positions on the team. It develops and nurtures

motivational characteristics based upon **'A what's in it for me' attitude** among participants."[62]

As a result, many players often become uptight, anxious, and fearful of making mistakes, knowing that if they are perceived as incompetent, they will not be selected. Furthermore, for many the primary objective of learning and experimenting with new skills is not even a consideration, as players feel as though they are being evaluated during every training session and game. Therefore, enjoyment levels, motivation, satisfaction, and the opportunity to develop as a player are reduced significantly.

Furthermore, this 'fight for a place' mentality encourages players to become envious and resentful when their teammates perform well or receive praise from others. Additionally, those players who want to be perceived as superior in comparison to their teammates publicly ridicule others who make mistakes in an attempt to move themselves up in the pecking order. Also, when things become challenging or the team is losing, players subjected to this ego focused environment invariably display increased levels of frustration and anger. To save face, these players will also frequently **blame their teammates for their own mistakes or misfortunes**. In their study investigating the motivational settings in youth soccer, researcher Professor Yngvar Ommundsen from the Norwegian School of Sport Sciences and his colleagues establish that these negative aspects merely fuel rivalry, conflict, and hostility among teammates.[63] Any clubs or coaches creating this setting with youngsters are clearly misguided or are not truly concerned about the players' development and welfare.

How minutes should be distributed

Coaches and parents must promote an inclusive environment where **all players** are treated equally and with upmost respect. And regardless of their current level of ability, all players must be provided with healthy amounts of playing time. Again, it is important to reiterate that this task is easier to accomplish when winning takes a backseat to learning and individual development.

For years we have emphasized to the young players in our program the notion that they will receive fair amounts of playing time. **They are not there to perform for us. We are there to help them develop and enjoy their learning experiences.** Therefore, we develop the understanding that a player's performance has no bearing on the amount of playing time they receive during their formative years.

Offering equal playing time to all players has a number of positive benefits. By doing this, players will be **free of the pressure and constraint** of trying to impress the coach to ensure that they receive playing time in the future. This will also fuel the healthy notion that utilizing the game as a tool to learn, improve, and simply enjoy their early soccer experiences is the main objective. Furthermore, affording all players equal playing time eradicates the perception that the team has a 'star player' on whom everyone relies and fuels a mentality that players of all ability can work communally to achieve their objectives. This contributes further towards creating a positive and harmonious environment because it dispels any potential contention among teammates.

Unconditionally receiving equal playing time also helps to reduce players' fear of any making mistakes, and therefore, their **self-esteem, motivation, and confidence levels become significantly elevated**, due to the fact they are permitted to express their creative talents without concern that they may lose playing time by making errors or having an 'off day', which is likely to occur when players are young.

Finally, coaches who provide players with equal playing time prevent unrest and ill feeling with the parents. For example, parents who realize that their child is not fighting with another player for a position on the field and whose child is receiving an equal amount of playing time become more relaxed and have far more trust in the coach's principles. Naturally, parent-to-parent interaction is enhanced considerably because all players are treated with equal respect regardless of their current capabilities. This positively impacts the overall environment for young players, which in turn helps to improve their immediate soccer experiences, the chances of them remaining in the sport, and the likelihood of them progressing more effectively in the long term.

Chapter Five

Identifying Talent and Potential

"Appropriate development must be prioritized over the all too common drive for early success, where selection procedures focus predominantly on winning."[64]

Dr. Russ Martindale et al, 2007

During our research we spoke to many elite coaches who work for various English Premier League clubs and who have the responsibility of developing young talent for the future. In our discussions, these coaches stressed the difficult nature of predicting which players would go on to the professional level.

For example, they emphasized how often they have been surprised by players who seemingly had it all at an early age, only to be released and not offered a contract later in their teens. Conversely, they also accentuated how many young players progressed significantly after puberty (players in this scenario are often referred to as 'late developers') and went on to be top professional players.

A look at the story of Paul Scholes when he was in the earlier stages of his development will demonstrate this point. This player has undoubtedly been one of the greatest players in Manchester United's history and is regarded as one of the finest international midfielders of all time. However, former Manchester United Academy Director and Chief Scout Les Kershaw points out that the story could have been very different:

He couldn't run. He was a little one. Had asthma. No strength or power. No athleticism. No endurance. 'You've got a dwarf,' someone said to Brian Kidd (former Manchester United Youth Team Coach). 'You will eat your words,' said Brian Kidd. If Scholesy had been at a lesser club they would have **got rid of him** and he would probably not be in the game now. We stuck with Scholesy, a wonderful technician.[65]

Coming through the playing ranks at Blackpool Football Club, we observed scenarios such as this first hand. For example, players who were not as advanced as others when they were young, and who often received limited recognition from coaches and parents, became successful soccer players in the long-term. Looking back now, clearly a number of these players were simply late developers and started to flourish significantly later as teenagers. We were happy to see that they reached the elite levels of the professional game in the U.K.

On the other hand, we also played alongside a number of individuals who clearly displayed advanced capabilities when they were in their early teens. Predictably, these players were being lauded as the next 'big thing', and many coaches and parents quickly made the assumption that they would 'make it' to the professional level. However, after maturation these players seemingly fell behind other players and were not being spoken about in the same light as they were previously. Unfortunately, many of these players discontinued their involvement in soccer.

These experiences help us to understand and appreciate how there are many variables that can determine a young players' future in the game. For example, the players' desire to learn, level of intelligence, social background, and personality traits are just a few variables to consider besides their physical, technical, and tactical capabilities. Furthermore, when we take into account that many young players experience considerable fluctuations throughout their maturation, we can appreciate why predicting which players are going to be successful in the future is a **complex and arduous task.**

This point is also recognized by many leading researchers involved in youth development. Craig Simmons, the Player Development Advisor for the English Football Association, offers his thoughts on this issue:

Establishing one player's status across many developmental parameters is difficult, but imagine the impossible task of trying to create an exact science which has to take into account the impact of numerous and ever changing maturational factors in each player.[66]

Simmons' message clearly highlights how difficult it would be to create an exact science behind identifying future talent. What clouds this issue even further in youth soccer is that many coaches and administrators consistently base their predictions of future talent on subjective opinion and intuition, **which are often proven to be very unreliable**. A number of researchers have expressed their concerns about such an approach. For example, in their study investigating the role of maturity status on talent identification in soccer, sport scientist César Meylan and colleagues substantiate this perception whey they state:

> The 'coach-driven' method of talent identification rests on intuitive knowledge comprised of socially constructed images of the perfect player. Choices of gifted players are therefore made on personal taste and this process is viewed as legitimate by coaches. However, such an approach is highly subjective and can lead to repetitive misconceptions in talent evaluation.[67]

Unfortunately, as many clubs and coaches throughout the U.S. take an approach where the primary objective is winning during the players' formative years, the reality is that they are not dedicated to players' development and long-term potential: **They are devoted to identifying players who can produce performances which will help them in their quest to meet this objective.**

We will now look at three facets of how talent is customarily identified by many coaches and parents in U.S. youth soccer.

Relative Age Effect and Early Development

Traditionally, U.S. youth soccer utilizes chronological age to brand players and teams into age groups and divisions. For example, the 'soccer year' begins August 1st and ends July 31st; therefore a player born on August 9th, 2002 will be categorized in the same age group as a player born on July 26th, 2003.

Therefore, players could be almost a year older in age than other players in their chronological group, which can result in significant physical and psychological advancement, and in many cases it means these players have more experience in the sport, all of which has the potential to offer players initial performance advantages. This concept is referred to as the **'Relative Age Effect'**[68] and **many clubs and coaches inappropriately capitalize on this situation to the fullest extent.**

Significant research establishes that initial performance advantages, due to relative age effect, are a key factor in many age categories. For example, when researcher Dr. Werner Helsen and his colleagues investigated relative age effect and dropout in youth soccer, they discovered that even at the U7 – U9 age groups relative age effect was prevalent, with players predominantly born in August, September, and October being selected for teams due to the performance advantages they had to offer.[69] Additionally, Professor Francis Glamser and Dr. John Vincent investigated whether the relative age effect was prevalent in the U.S. Olympic Development Program[70] and in a group of elite youth soccer players.[71] In both cases, they established the relative age effect was prevalent and, in respect to the ODP Program, they discovered it was particularly apparent among male state, regional and national players.

Aside from players having initial performance advantages due to being born earlier in the soccer year, obviously some players will be early developers and therefore may be bigger, stronger, faster, and demonstrate psychological advancement in comparison to their peers. But whether it is a case of relative age effect or early growth, a major mistake many coaches and parents make during the players' early stages of development is immediately identifying those players who possess physical advantages as the more talented ones. Just because certain players display this dominance at the younger age does not mean that they are the individuals who possess the talent, neither does it definitively signal that they are going to have success in the future. Professor Renaat Philippaerts and colleagues looked into the relationship between peak height velocity and physical performance in youth soccer players and concluded that:

In the context of talent identification and development, trainers and coaches should recognize that changes in growth and performance are highly individualized. **In the context of long-term talent development, the best performers in adulthood were not necessarily early maturing players.**[72]

These initial performance advantages due to advanced physical attributes are like **gold dust** to such clubs and coaches primarily focusing on winning and trophy hunting. In our research we spoke with several directors at self-proclaimed leading youth clubs in the U.S. who clearly stipulated that identifying and attracting the best players during the early stages of development was crucial for their quest to win games and be successful. Again, many club administrators and coaches are fully aware that parents and players are likely to migrate to their organization if they are winning at all age groups; hence the reason for so much promotion of trophy success on club websites.

Here is a very common scenario in U.S. youth soccer:

Johnny is 13 years old and physically big, fast, and strong for his age due to maturing early. His coach clearly knows that he can just power his way through the opposing defense and score goals. **Therefore, he encourages the team to get the ball to him so he can do just that. During the season, Johnny scores many goals and his team wins the league. Many parents think Johnny is an incredible athlete who will undoubtedly be a great player in the future!**

Clearly here, the coach is taking full advantage of the players' physical attributes in order to make his team successful. However, selecting and utilizing players in this manner frequently results in negative ramifications in both the short and long-term. A couple of key examples demonstrate this point.

First, an obvious flaw in this approach is that, in the short-term, players who are physically smaller and weaker or born later in the calendar year are often neglected or not afforded the same playing opportunities. Alarmingly, this is regularly the case even with smaller and weaker players who demonstrate **advanced levels of technical ability and game understanding**. Dr. Helsen and colleagues highlight this point in their study investigating the relative age effect in youth soccer when they state, "Players who are less developed physically because of their younger relative age, but who are talented or more technically gifted, are clearly not selected compared with those born earlier in the year."[73]

We must understand that less physically advanced players who are not selected or offered much playing time may not have the capability of understanding that this predicament can often change in the future. This is especially the case when coaches fail to relay this important message to young players who develop and mature later. Therefore, many players faced with this scenario naturally begin to question if they are 'good enough', suffer from low self-perceived competence, and become self-conscious about their size. Maybe it would be good practice to remind these youngsters that one of the greatest soccer players of all time, **Diego Maradona**, was only a mere **5 foot 5 inches**, and arguably the greatest player of the modern era, **Lionel Messi**, stands only at **5 foot 7 inches!** But regardless of these facts, numerous young players who perceive themselves as not meeting the physical requirements lose interest in the sport and in many cases drop out altogether, before they have received the opportunity and 'right' to explore their potential.

Second, those players who have performance advantages at the early stages of development due to being physically bigger, stronger, or born earlier in the calendar year often face developmental problems in the future. This is because many are encouraged at a young age to **repeatedly utilize their physical traits** in order to help clubs and coaches win games during a critical time in their development, a time when it is **crucial** for them to practice **important skills** and develop creative aspects of the game for their long-term progression. Unfortunately, many young players subjected to this scenario experience problems during their later teenage years when their **technical deficiencies are exposed** and when their physical advantages are no longer present due to others catching up in the physical growth process.

This viewpoint is substantiated by researchers Dr. Matthew Pain and Jimenez who investigated wasted potential in youth soccer due to the relative age effect. They demonstrate how the advantages afforded to comparatively bigger, stronger players often leads them to deemphasize the development of important skills required in the game. Therefore, in the later stages of their development, when the physical advantages they once had due to the relative age effect have diminished, these players lack key skills, resulting in their **failing to compete with peers whom they used to dominate**, especially as those physically inferior players spent crucial time working on skill development when these physically bigger individuals did not.[74]

Conversely, those players without physical advantages early in their development must rely more on attributes such as technical skill, the ability to change direction quickly, creativity, awareness, and their decision making capacity. So, if these players are able to maintain their involvement into their later teenage years, these critical attributes are often far more advanced in contrast to those players who failed to spend the necessary time working on these key areas due to their coaches relying solely on their physical advantages at a young age.

The important issue once again is that many self-proclaimed leading clubs and organizations who utilize initial performance advantages actually **claim long-term player development is their primary objective.** This is another classic contradiction made by so many. If they truly focused on the long-term development of players they certainly would not take advantage of the relative age effect and/or players' physical attributes merely to win at the cost of discarding or neglecting players who fail to possess such innate physical prowess during their early years. They would be offering everyone equal opportunities to develop their potential in the long-term. Clearly these clubs are misguided or they are deliberately misleading players and parents due to ulterior motives.

*Here are two **U12 players** of similar technical ability. However, due to his physical advantages, many clubs and coaches would select the player on the right and pigeonhole him in the center of defense to increase the team's chances of winning.*

Tryouts

A popular method used by many to identify talent is the traditional tryout procedure. Over the years, even in regard to young children, parents interested in our program have commonly asked, *"When are your tryouts?"*. Our response to this question is **"Why should young players in the early stages of their development have to tryout to enjoy playing or learn the game of soccer?"**. Although this is another traditional process unwaveringly repeated by many youth soccer coaches and organizations throughout the U.S., it is flawed on many levels from a developmental perspective.

We investigated several clubs *(including travel teams and self-affirmed leading organizations)* that discussed how even at the younger age groups the tryout procedure was crucial in identifying the '**best players**'. Remarkably, some of these clubs emphasize on their websites how these tryouts can be 'stressful' for players, since their abilities are scrutinized under pressure and many who fail to demonstrate the required level of performance will **be cut**. But highlighting this point confirms their awareness of the negative ramifications of such settings.

Why would clubs and organizations ever subject young players to such a traumatic setting if they were truly concerned about young people's development? Of course, as players progress into their teens, performing under pressure is an important component of becoming an effective player. However, we must remember we are talking about young children in the earliest stages of their involvement who simply want to get out and play without constraint or pressure. But immediately they are subjected to tryouts and placed under the stress of having to perform just to receive the opportunity to participate in the sport!

The problems with these tryouts are caused again by many clubs and administrators only looking for players who can perform right now. For example, the major problem is that many young players get cut and are simply sent the message, **"You are not good enough!".** When young players are subjected to this naturally they are more likely to lose interest and in many cases drop out of the sport altogether simply because they are led to believe that soccer is not for them due to being no good at the game. This philosophy fails to explore potential and translates to **"If you're a late developer, forget it! We only want players who can help us win this season!".**

But what is this evaluation of being good enough based on? It is centered on how players **compare** to others at the tryout. Of course many young players will naturally look at how they match up to their peers in terms of capability, which can often lead to dejection and self-doubt if players feel inferior, and can also lead to complacency for players who perceive themselves as superior. However, as players cannot control how others perform and develop and can only influence their own progress and destiny, fueling an environment where player comparisons are the decisive factor is a big mistake made by coaches and parents. We must reiterate that at a young age players need to immerse themselves in their self-improvement and measure success on their personal progression. But this tryout procedure immediately promotes young players to make assessments based on how they compare to their teammates.

Nevertheless, as this method has been used for years, many clubs and coaches just continue on repeating it without question. But these negative ramifications certainly contribute as to why numerous development experts and leading figures advocate that clubs and coaches **should not do tryouts during the early stages of development.** For example, in the current U.S. Youth Soccer Player Development Model which was released in 2012, it emphasizes how there should be **no tryouts** during these critical periods of young players' experiences.[75]

Of course, there are always going to be those 'old school' thinkers who adamantly believe that 'it's a tough world out there' and that attending a tryout regardless of the end result will provide a valuable lesson for their child. There are also those parents who place their own self-interests ahead of their child's, loving the drama of the tryout procedure and the chance to see how their child compares to the rest. However, coaches with clipboards trying to identify which players to cut and which players can make them successful today are **totally misguided** if they believe that they are involved in true player development.

Recruiting for winning

For many clubs the incessant quest for impact players does not end after the tryout. Throughout the season it is very common for clubs to pursue the ones they identify as the best players from other organizations. Of course, there will always be those players who possess excellent technical ability, physical advantages, decision making capabilities, and game understanding at the earliest of ages; **and any layman can simply gather talented players to put on a team and win games during the early stages of development.**

Over the years, we have experienced many players in our program being recruited by trophy hunting clubs which know that the services of these players will help them achieve their objectives. Frequently it is a coach attempting to entice a player to their organization. But in many cases parents go above and beyond to recruit players in an effort to strengthen their child's team to fulfill their own short-term aspirations.

This recent example demonstrates a typical scenario we have repeatedly encountered:

*A 10 year old training in our development program begins to attract significant interest from self-proclaimed leading clubs in the area. He is a very talented boy, clearly gifted athletically, and making excellent progress. But crucially, **he is really enjoying his soccer experiences in our environment**. After an attempt is made to recruit him by a local club, the parents inform us that they were predictably told, **"Your son needs to be with us! Our club is the best place for development and that's our focus. We travel to the best tournaments in the country! If your child doesn't get this level of competition now, he won't be able to compete later! We can make him a great player!!"***

Such recruitment scenarios are worthy of analysis. Here is a 10 year player learning and progressing well, confirmed by the club's admiration and interest in recruiting him. But crucially this player is enjoying his soccer experiences in his present environment. In light of this, what seems irrational is that these clubs claim that they care about young people and their development. If this were truly the case, the first task they would carry out would be to determine whether the child was happy and enjoying his or her soccer experiences, and as soon as they realized that the player was happy, these clubs and coaches would leave the player alone and without disruption at such a young age. But this is regularly disregarded by recruiters who only consider what the young player can do for them in their quest for short-term success, irrespective of the potential negative ramifications this will have for the young players experience in the sport.

Although many parents may feel happy or proud that their child is wanted, it is crucial that they recognize why this is happening and identify what the true recruiting motives are, because again **it is commonly the case of what the player can do for the club, not what the club can do for the player**. One of our objectives is to encourage more parents with this process and help them understand why individuals from other clubs are coming to them for their children, or as is often the case **their child's 'services'**.

Therefore, being equipped with some fundamental knowledge as to why they are being approached in the first place and having the ability to identify the signs which help determine the club's, coaches', or parents' motives can be extremely helpful. Here are some useful questions to ask someone when they try to recruit or encourage you to have your child join their club or team:

- *Why do you want my child to join your organization?*
- *How do you measure success?*
- *What is your main objective as a coach, team, or club?*
- *What do you differently which will help develop my child effectively?*
- *What is your approach to games?*

We must be aware that coaches and parents will consistently provide *generic responses* to these questions espousing what is best for player development, **often making no sense whatsoever**. Let's use the first question in the following scenario to outline the misleading responses many coaches demonstrate and are regularly not held accountable for.

*A coach from a self-proclaimed leading organization approaches you and hands over a **"You have been identified"** card because they spotted your child playing well in a recent game. So you exchange phone numbers and a couple of days later he gives you a call.*

*After some initial discussion in which he highlights all the tournaments and trophies his teams have won you ask him, **"Why do you want my child to join your organization?"***

*Recruiting coach: "Errrrr, because we're the **best** place for player development and we can help develop your child's potential!"*

Parent: "Well, that doesn't really answer my question. Let me put it another way. **Why are you so concerned about my child's welfare?"**

Recruiting coach: "Well, errrrrrr, we pride ourselves on offering the **best** *players in this area the chance to play on teams which face the* **best** *competition. And we travel out of state to the* **best** *tournaments, because we want to produce the* **best** *players we can".*

Parent: "Well, again, you've not really answered my question. Anyway, **why is it so important for my child to face the best competition and travel all over to tournaments at such a young age?"**

Recruiting coach: "Well, to be the **best** *you've gotta play against the* **best** *at the* **best** *tournaments! We must challenge players at a high level if we want them to be great players!"* **Everyone knows that!** *If they're not traveling out of state and playing in the* **best** *tournaments against the* **best** *players, they're gonna miss out!"*

Parent: "Well that's interesting because I recently read how the U.S. soccer directors are opposed to all this out of state tournament travel with young players. I also read that focusing solely on winning trophies should never be the main objective with young players. **What do you think of this?"**

Recruiting coach: "Well, I'm not sure what directors you're referring to, there are obviously many philosophies out there. Anyway, let me make it clear, we only go to these tournaments so we can face the **best** *competition, our focus at this club isn't on winning trophies; it's on player development!" And that's why we develop the* **best** *players!*

Parent: Well, that's interesting cause **the first thing you told me was how many state cups and trophies your club has won.** *Furthermore, after you gave me the 'Your child has been identified card'* **I went to your website and I immediately observed how it was plastered with trophies and tournament success even at the earliest of age groups!** *Anyway, I don't think it's the right place for my child. Thanks for your time.*

As we can see in this common scenario the answers were generic and failed to get to the heart of the parent's original question. This is a classic case of a façade masking the coach or club's true objectives. But we have regularly questioned why these clubs do not announce with conviction that their genuine objective is finding the best players to win as many trophies as possible. Then they could approach parents and say, **"We would like your child to join our club because we feel they are someone who can help us win trophies and be successful."** Although from a development perspective this is the wrong approach, from an **ethical viewpoint** it is a far more appropriate path to take and would certainly cause less confusion in U.S. youth soccer. But instead, what we see are many clubs and organizations hiding their true motives behind the pdf files and coaching articles posted on their websites which were relayed to them by their State and National Directors who are working hard to implement suitable recommendations to improve player development.

Arguably one of the most critical points of this recruitment for winning process is when coaches attempting to bring in 'better talent' do so at the expense of players currently on the roster who often get cut and are told that their services are no longer required. This creates a significant point of contention which we have often questioned. How can these clubs, coaches, and parents be taken seriously when they use **'team unity'** and **'team camaraderie'** as incentives to entice a player into their club but then remove players from the current roster to complete this process? Where is the team unity and camaraderie in saying to a young player, **"Sorry, you have to go somewhere** *else now as we have players coming in who are currently better than you who will improve our chances of winning."*

This common behavior supports the thoughts of many leading figures in youth soccer and elite development experts who indicate how so many organizations spend far too much time figuring out how to recruit players into their club rather than spending the energy on developing their own players. These organizations know if a player in their program is failing to perform then they can just bring in someone else! As athletic development expert Kelvin Giles affirms, "Sports teams that operate academies and other talent recruitment systems should **consider the difference between recruiting a player and developing a player."**[76]

Of course it makes perfect sense for those misguided clubs, coaches, and parents who place the main emphasis on winning and accumulating as many trophies as possible to deliberately capitalize on young players' advantageous physical attributes, implement tryouts, and actively recruit those whom they perceive to be the best players. However, this *'you'll do us for now'* mentality and the indisputable focus on what a player can do for the club not what the club can do for the player comes at a high cost for young players and youth soccer in the U.S.

Whether it is relative age effect, tryouts, or recruiting, we must understand that these conventional talent identification procedures focus primarily on physical attributes and fail to take into account many long term developmental considerations to allow future potential to flourish. We must consider how studies indicate that decision making, awareness, and players' creativity are actually better indicators to predict future talent. Research by sports psychologist Torbjörn Vestberg and colleagues investigating the decisive indicators that predict success in soccer concluded that **cognitive processes, which they term as executive functions (e.g. decision making, problem solving and creative thinking), are actually more effective determinants of predicting future success.**[77] These findings reinforce the view (discussed in chapter two 'Sideline Instruction') that we must allow players the chance to develop their decision-making skills and problem solving capabilities during their early years.

Unfortunately, these findings are often not considered by many involved in U.S. youth soccer, and the result is numerous cases of wasted potential as players are **ruthlessly evaluated** and determined as not being good enough at this precise moment in comparison to those players who possess the favorable physical attributes. So, in essence, not only are coaches taking the wrong approach during the early stages of development by prematurely judging how good a player is going to be in the future, but the assessment criteria they use is often flawed. Clearly this is another case where many clubs and coaches who are not primarily concerned with players' wellbeing and development **can't even do it wrong right!**

A Positive Approach

If we want **more** players to enjoy the sport, continue their participation, and unlock their true potential in their future years we must alter the conventional mindset on identifying talent and instead embrace potential in the correct manner.

First, clubs and coaches must **stop** utilizing young players' talent and physical advantages merely to win games and obtain short-term accolades. They must approach games from the learning perspective we described in chapter one.

Second, we must always remember that everyone has potential and that players can often surprise us in their development, considering they will grow, mature, and learn at different rates regardless of the ability or physical capabilities they demonstrate today. As author James T McCay proclaims, **"No matter what the level of your ability, you have more potential than you can ever develop in a lifetime."**[78] Therefore, we must place the primary focus on what the player could do in the future (a long-term approach) and not on what the player can do today (a short-term approach).

By following a long-term vision which involves patience, sensible progression, and realistic expectations, we will undoubtedly offer a higher percentage of young players an opportunity to enjoy, learn, and develop a passion for the game. This in turn allows us to retain more players in the sport which must always be our primary goal during the early stages of the players' development.

Over the past decade we have emphasized to coaches and parents how development must be viewed from a long-term perspective. We have worked with many young players who have demonstrated various levels of ability and individual differences, making our role in soccer both enjoyable and challenging. Throughout the years we have observed the following types of players:

- *Players who progress steadily during their early developmental years.*

- *Players who find the early stages of their soccer experiences a little trickier due to their physical and psychological genetics and often require increased levels of positive support.*

- *Players who appear to be developing very well one minute and struggling the next, only to be seemingly doing well again in a short amount of time.*

- *Players who appear advanced for their age* (these players are considered 'impact players' by many clubs and coaches who often attempt to recruit them for their own benefit).

- *Players who display amazing technical, physical, tactical, and psychological capabilities at such a young age that they stand out remarkably* (again, these players are heavily recruited).

Regardless of which category a player may fall into, we have commonly observed many parents falling into the trap of becoming overly excited or too concerned about their child's performance levels at an early age. Many will often compare their child's abilities to those players of similar age in an effort to gauge where there child stands in the 'pecking order'. Although this may seem a natural and relatively harmless process for parents to undertake, it actually causes a considerable amount of unnecessary stress and concern and can be detrimental to their child's progress and participation if relayed to the child.

For example, parents have approached us with their thoughts and concerns regarding their child's performance often making statements such as: **"He's really playing well lately!"**; or conversely, if their child's performance level has dipped, many will ask, **"Can I get a few minutes of your time? I have some concerns about my child's play."**

When this situation arises, we always inform parents that becoming overly concerned with performance levels or attempting to evaluate how they are doing in comparison to other players is futile, as the players' progress and performance levels will again commonly fluctuate throughout their formative years. In her study investigating parental relationships in youth sports, Associate Professor Thelma Horn of Miami University supports this viewpoint by pointing out:

> If coaches provide parents with information about the varying rates of maturation and their temporary effects on youth-sports participants' performance, then parents' concerns about their child's current 'place' in the peer comparison structure maybe somewhat be alleviated.[79]

Furthermore, as games are being primarily used for learning, we remind any parents demonstrating impatience or unease that their child is neither being evaluated nor required to perform at a certain level. In these circumstances we alleviate parental concern by informing them to relax, display patience, and ask them to consider the following questions:

- *Is your child enjoying themselves?*
- *Are they experimenting and learning?*
- *Do they seem to be developing a passion for the game?*

If they answer "yes" to these questions, then the player is doing great! It also means that there is a high likelihood that we are creating a good environment for the player and increasing the chance of retaining the player in the sport. Helping parents understand these concepts is both positive and beneficial. Furthermore, the fact that researchers and development experts are discussing the need to relieve parents' concerns about their child's current 'place' and performances in comparison to their child's peers substantiates the point that parents do not need to be concerned about this in the first place.

We must remember that it is just as important to remind young players that they will likely experience a lot of changes over the upcoming years and that they need to remember **the focus is on their long-term development**. Therefore, they should not be overly concerned about their performance levels or how they compare to other players now. A way to say this so that young players easily understand is something along the lines of:

> *Remember, we're more concerned with your ability to play great soccer when you're older. So practicing skills now is the key. Use games and training to try things and be creative. If things go wrong, or you make a mistake, or you feel like you didn't play that well, or you feel like you're not as good as someone else, don't worry! Things will likely change! As long as you try your utmost and keep learning you'll have the best shot at being the best you can be!*

When players know that the focus is on their future development they are naturally more relaxed and more likely to develop a learner's mindset. **Players develop an understanding that they are working towards their future, which in turn helps them to capitalize on their true capabilities.**

The process of picking bananas is a useful analogy for coaches and parents to think about. Currently, the selection criterion that many youth soccer coaches adhere to in U.S. youth soccer is based on selecting the ripest, yellow bananas. However, rather than selecting the ripest, yellow bananas at the present time, youth soccer coaches must acknowledge the fact that the green bananas may also develop into something rather special too, if given the chance! As researchers Professor Ken Davids and colleagues point out in their investigation on talent identification and skill acquisition in soccer, **"Although coaches often make judgments about a player's talent, the decision should be based on the potential of that player to succeed following some developmental program, not on his or her ability to contribute to winning a match at one instant in time."**[80]

In reference to these considerations, we must make it very clear that we are not saying every single player will become the next soccer superstar like Lionel Messi, Wayne Rooney, or Cristiano Ronaldo. We are simply saying that every player should be offered the chance to demonstrate their true potential in the long-term and not be written off at a young age when they should be receiving the opportunity to enjoy and learn the sport.

A success story which emphasizes this viewpoint comes from a personal experience in our early coaching days. While working for the academy at Blackpool Football Club, an inexperienced coaching director was appointed and immediately expressed how the U9 players which we had invited to the club were simply not good enough. He then stressed the urgent need to 'get rid' of all these players and recruit better youngsters into the club.

Although we were young coaches at the time, even then, this quick evaluation seemed rash, unfair, and unreasonable. Interestingly, several of these young players have gone on to play professionally, including Michael Hall, who signed a professional contract with Blackburn Rovers in the English Premier League, and Mark Halstead, who made his Premier League debut against Chelsea in 2011. **It is no surprise that this coaching director in question did not last long in his role!**

Many elite coaches take a positive approach towards identifying future talent, importantly recognizing that major fluctuations will always occur in young players' performance levels during the early stages of their development. Dr. Russ Martindale and colleagues, investigating the perspectives of elite coaches in the U.K on the issue of effective talent development, provide the insightful views of two leading coaches:

Coach A: "I think it's very important at developmental level that you don't write off the ones who aren't there yet, because you will find 12 months will change things dramatically."

Coach B: "I think we have to be careful. I have seen people who have developed and then stood still for 2 or 3 years and then things have kicked in and they have developed again. It's just how things go and develop and who knows what is going to happen."[81]

This point is reaffirmed by Dr. Christine Nash and colleagues who investigated elite sports coaches' philosophies. One particular elite coach who was interviewed in this study emphasized an important point when working with young players, **"Always you should look when you are coaching at what you want them to be at age 18 - it's not important what they are doing now and a lot of parents get caught up in that."**[82]

Furthermore, in his article for <u>The New York Times</u> entitled 'How a Soccer Star is Made', Michael Sokolove discusses visiting the renowned youth academy of Ajax Amsterdam, in the Netherlands, to elicit the ideas and philosophy of coaches working with, arguably, the most effective and productive youth systems in European soccer. One of the individuals Sokolove interviewed for this particular article was Ronald de Jong who undertakes scouting duties for the Ajax youth academy. He summarized his view on how he identifies potential talent by stating that,

I am never looking for a result – for example, which player is scoring the most goals or even who is running the fastest. **That may be because of their size and stage of development**. Does the player have creativity with the ball? Does it seem like they are loving the game? I think these things are good at predicting how he'll be when he is older. [83]

In the scenario earlier in this chapter where the coach solely relied upon his player's physical attributes to score lots of goals, we demonstrated how players with physical advantages or certain talents are encouraged to use those qualities so that clubs and coaches can win things today. We will now look at the same scenario, but we will demonstrate how this situation is managed differently by elite coaches who harbor a long-term developmental perspective:

Johnny is 13 years old and physically big, fast, and strong for his age due to maturing early. His coach clearly knows that he can just power his way through the opposing defense and score goals. **However, as he is primarily concerned about developing players' future potential and not on winning games and short-term success, he understands that encouraging him just to use these physical advantages will not develop his all-round game. Therefore, while placing Johnny in various positions on the field, he encourages him to try and be creative with the ball, working on skills which will help his touch and overall development.**

The approach from this coach is obviously a clear contrast to the one earlier. This coach understands that he could utilize Johnny's abilities and physical advantages to help his team win and be successful today, but he is more interested in Johnny's long-term development and potential than in what Johnny can do for him or the team right now.

We must make it clear that we are not stating that young players who possess such advantages should not be able to use those strengths. Of course, soccer is a physically demanding sport, and certainly it can be beneficial when players possess innate physical capabilities. But the key point is that **coaches must not hammer players to exclusively rely upon these physical advantages time and time again to help the team win now, they must encourage youngsters to develop their all-round game so they will be better players in the future.**

When it comes to talent identification and potential, sports psychologist Sir John Whitmore encapsulates the message we have tried to convey in this chapter in his book <u>Coaching for Performance</u>: **"We are more like acorns, each of which contains within it all the potential to be a magnificent oak tree. We need nourishment, encouragement, and the light to reach toward, but the oaktreeness is already within us."**[84]

Chapter Six

Challenging Players Appropriately

"Youngsters should be presented with challenges that suit their current abilities, interests, and expectations. Those challenges should be like their shoes: They should fit perfectly and be comfortable."[85]

Horst Wein – Author and elite youth soccer coach

In order for young players to enjoy their experience, maintain their passion for the sport, and enhance their learning opportunities, it is essential to provide them with appropriate challenges during games and training. Undoubtedly, getting this balance right for every player can be difficult and therefore it is a process requiring significant deliberation. For sake of clarity, in this chapter we will limit the discussion to the challenges players face **during games.**

Before we proceed, we must briefly mention the concept of 'readiness', a crucial consideration when working with young players. Dr. Sally Harris of the Palo Alto Medical Foundation defines readiness as, "A process in which an individual child's cognitive, social and motor development is evaluated to determine whether the child can meet the demands [of the sporting scenario they face]."[86]

Because of the many developmental variables we need to consider, the key is presenting optimal challenges that do not overwhelm players due to their difficulty, or offering challenges which are too easy and result in their becoming disinterested or discouraged. So, before we throw players into any sporting situation, we must consider whether they are ready from these developmental perspectives.

Interestingly, parents often ask teachers, principals, family members, and friends whether they believe their child is ready to meet the demands of various activities and subjects. One example is how parents will commonly ask, "Is my child ready for school?", regularly taking into account their child's mental, emotional, social, and physical maturity in the process. However, when it comes to youth soccer, many coaches and parents fail to take this approach. In her discussion on cooperation versus competition, Dr. Ann Michelle Daniels of South Dakota State University asserts, "In the context of organized sports, such questions occur much less frequently, if at all. If parents do seek information from others on their child's readiness, it rarely goes beyond physical aptitude, such as asking whether their child is 'too small' to compete on the soccer field."[87]

But due to a conventional approach taken by high numbers of clubs and organizations throughout the U.S. where teams are put together at a young age and the emphasis is placed on short-term results, many young players are not challenged appropriately during games, resulting in detrimental consequences both in the short-term and in the future. From our observations and experiences, a major aspect as to why many players are inappropriately challenged is due to **many coaches and parents mistakenly believing that constantly pushing and challenging players beyond their capabilities will simply make them better. This misguided belief is supported by no empirical evidence.**

Then why is this belief so passionately adhered to? First, it is customarily promoted by coaches and parents through sweeping statements such as *"Playing against better players makes you better"* or *"You must be challenged at the 'highest level' if you want to improve."* These statements are repeated time and time again by adults who offer **limited consideration** about what they are saying and why they believe it. However, such empirically unsupported declarations are easily challenged by simply asking the proclaimer, *"What makes you believe that?"*, to which they often respond with a statement such as, *"Well, everyone knows that!".*

Unfortunately, such ambiguous statements leave both coaches and parents harboring a strong desire for **all young players** to be pushed beyond their limits, irrespective of their readiness and their progressive needs. Mistakenly, many parents fear the consequences of not pushing their child into high levels of challenge when they are young thinking that they will 'miss the boat' and fall behind everyone. But as we will demonstrate, due to the diverse capabilities and necessities of each individual, some players will benefit from a level of challenge that would be unsuitable for the progressive needs of another. However, because coaches and parents see one player having developmental success, they incorrectly assume the same demands at that level are effective in the development of every player. Former Olympic coach, Kelvin Giles, dispels this notion stating, "Each player presents a unique set of variables that must be considered. A coach may be faced with a large group of athletes, but **'one size does not fit all.'**"[88]

Additionally, many young players are consistently thrust into overly challenging situations because their coaches and parents fail to display the necessary **patience** that the development process requires. It is very common for adults to crave immediate results, often displaying frustration and impatience when they fail to obtain them. Therefore, accompanied by misguided belief, this further increases the urgency to rush young players into challenges they are not ready for as many coaches and parents simply believe it will quickly make players more effective. But as leading youth soccer coach Horst Wein affirms, **"Nature does not take short cuts; there is a natural, unhurried order to it all. Coaches, parents, and administrators should copy nature's wisdom."**[89]

To facilitate our understanding of how players are repeatedly challenged inappropriately and demonstrate how we can provide young players with challenges that enhance their development, we will utilize three common scenarios which surface frequently in youth soccer.

Scenario 1: Players being pushed beyond their capabilities

*While playing for her local U10 travel team, Sally, 9 years old, begins to demonstrate an increased passion for the game. As her team only practices once a week and plays one game at the weekends, Sally tells her parents that she would like to do more. So, without much investigation her parents decide to take her to the tryout at a premier club in the area. Although Sally lacks technical skill and her ball control is something she finds difficult to cope with **even when she is under no***

pressure from an opponent, *she exhibits good speed and physical size. From a psychological perspective she has a calm and determined character. However, it is Sally's physical attributes that the coaches immediately identify as being **advantageous for their team in terms of winning games and being successful**. Therefore, she is offered a place on the roster, and Sally's parents inform her travel team coach that she will no longer be playing for them as she made the tryout.*

During her first game against high level competition, her parents immediately recognize that the play is much quicker in comparison to the level she previously played at with her old team. Consequently, Sally finds it very difficult to cope with the demands of the game. Struggling to control the ball and execute other basic techniques, Sally frequently loses possession (to the disapproval of her coach and other parents on the sideline). Due to this, Sally appears to be uptight and begins to demonstrate a lack of willingness to want the ball.

With the score tied and the end of the game drawing near, the ball is passed to Sally who makes a mistake, and the opposing player races through on goal and scores. The coach aggressively yells onto the field, **"You can't let that happen! You have to be ready! You've got to get rid of the ball quicker."**

After the game Sally's Father approaches the coach (who is being paid for his services) to elicit his feelings about how she did. The coach responds:

*She found it difficult. But if we are going to compete against these teams **we need** her speed on defense to stop their forwards and she needs to get rid of the ball much quicker! If she just gets rid of the ball in that last play we tie that game. You have to remember we are playing against the best teams in* *the region - It's much tougher than what she's used to! And some games are gonna be even tougher than this! But this is what she needs - **she must face this type of competition every week in order to take her game to the 'next level'!***

During the ride home Sally, subdued and dejected, informs her parents that she did not enjoy playing and that she feels that she is not good enough to play at this level. But her father, who has been 'reassured' by the coach, conveys to Sally that she will be fine and must play against this type of 'high level' competition every week if she wants to improve.

This scenario which demonstrates a player being thrust into a game situation they are not ready for is a very common one in U.S. youth soccer. Before we look at the ramifications, we must remind ourselves of some critical points:

- *Sally is only 9 years of age and in the **early stages of development.***

- *She showed a desire to increase her participation in the sport, **not a desire to be challenged beyond her capabilities.***

- *She has significant technical limitation and struggles to control the ball under no pressure.*

- *She has expressed that she did not enjoy her experience.*

- *She has already started to doubt her ability.*

- *She has shown signs of dejection and disinterest.*

- *The coach's behavior and actions suggest he is primarily focusing on producing a winning team and short-term outcomes, as he is mainly concerned about how Sally can help him and the team compete and not on how he and the team environment can help Sally's development. This is highlighted by his desire to utilize Sally's speed to stop opposing defenders and for her to get rid of the ball quicker. Additionally, he didn't deal with her mistake in a positive manner, and he has quickly labeled Sally a defender despite the fact that she is only 9 years old.*

The initial signs propose that this level of challenge **fails to meet the player's progressive needs** and that the coach's overall philosophy is not going to benefit this young player's development. Although Sally is equipped with good physical attributes and a sound temperament her lack of technical proficiency is clearly an issue. But even though the coach and parents realized that she found it very difficult, and despite Sally expressing subdued feelings about playing at this level, remarkably the coach and the parents **still** came to the conclusion that this was a **positive** situation and **crucial for her development!**

It's been our experience that many coaches and parents ignore key indicators that a child is not ready for a certain level of challenge. Incredibly, many adults dismiss what the child may be expressing emotionally simply because they think they know better. For example, many coaches and parents take an approach where they believe young players should just **'hang in there'** and **'tough it out'**, as eventually these players will magically 'get it' and start shining at this level. But the reality for young players consistently placed into situations like this is that they will encounter a number of developmental problems.

First, players with technical limitations who constantly face a challenge that is too demanding will not have enough time on the ball to execute and **practice** fundamental techniques such as getting the ball under control, dribbling, and finding a pass. **This is especially the case when players are pushed beyond their limits against the 'best competition' around when they are clearly not ready.**

As players progress through their development, the art of receiving the ball in tight situations under immediate pressure and dealing with it appropriately is essential. However, **we must make a clear distinction here**. Simply pushing players who lack a solid technical foundation or have little playing experience into this highly competitive environment week after week is not going to provide them with the opportunities to practice or even attempt these basic technical aspects of the game they so **desperately need to improve**.

It is again useful to compare the previous scenario to a school setting to highlight how illogical it really is. For example, if a young child is instructed to demonstrate their knowledge of Pythagoras Theorem in front of an audience before the youth has acquired an appreciation of fundamental math concepts, one could assume that most parents would be baffled by this logic. Yet in youth soccer such **unrealistic expectations** are repeatedly placed on young players without many coaches and parents considering the negative impact doing so will have.

Many players facing high levels of competition will also begin to suffer a lack of confidence. Because the challenge is too demanding, players are clearly more likely to make mistakes, and this is significantly evident when players lack a solid technical foundation. This process is something we have observed time and time again over the years and causes many players to become anxious, often showing no interest in receiving the ball due to being singled out, punished, or ridiculed for their poor play.

Furthermore, when players are pushed into levels of challenge beyond their capabilities and display incompetence among teammates who demonstrate higher levels of ability, these emotions can be increased further due to the criticism they receive from more advanced players. This is an issue we consistently observe when winning is being emphasized as a major objective with young players. In this setting, players frequently become frustrated at less advanced teammates because their incompetence comes at a high cost as the main objective of winning is hindered. This sentiment is supported in research by Professor Yngvar Ommundsen and his colleagues on peer relationships in youth soccer. Their study indicates that some players will direct derogatory comments due to being irritated, impatient, and angry at players who display inferior performance levels and cause the play to regularly break down.[90]

Can we really expect young players to enjoy their soccer experiences, maintain a passion for the sport, and develop as players if the challenges they face during their formative years cause them to feel incompetent, anxious, and dejected? Regularly exposing young players to the highest level of competition when they are not ready to face this degree of challenge will likely cause failure to enjoy the sport, limited development, a loss of interest, and ultimately cease participation. These observations are supported by Professor Csíkszentmihályi and his colleagues who established in their publication, <u>Talented Teenagers: the Roots of Success and Failure</u>, that many young individuals frequently drop out of sport due to the anxiety they experience **because their skill level was too low for the challenges they encountered**.[91]

So, if we want to take positive action in regards to Sally's development, the first step we must take is to **remove her out of this situation**. To reaffirm, Sally developed a passion due to her experiences and enjoyment from playing with her travel team at the previous level of challenge. She then demonstrated an interest to increase her participation in the sport. Again, she did not express the desire to be thrust into a highly competitive environment where the focus is on team success and the demands are currently beyond her capabilities, causing her stress and anxiety.

This course of action has been standard procedure for many parents. We have observed many young players being removed from positive environments they were enjoying and thrust into a highly competitive situation just because of the notion of *"Well, that's what you do"*. But again there is not much reflection on what is happening in this process and frequently many parents fall into the trap of fearing their child will miss out, especially if they have been informed by misguided 'rascals' that if their child doesn't face high level competition now and get on a team which travels to the biggest tournaments around that their child may as well forget it!

One of the best indicators of whether a child is receiving an appropriate level of challenge is establishing the child's own perspective on the situation. This important point is reaffirmed by Dr. Joel Brenner in a study undertaken for the American Academy of Pediatrics, "Ultimately, it is important to discuss the underlying motivation with the player. **It is best to identify and focus on the child's motivation to provide guidance.**"[92] However, the opinions and feelings of young players is often overlooked, which was clearly the case in the scenario when Sally expressed her emotions in the car ride home.

So instead of simply ignoring what the child feels and hijacking their path in the sport due to being influenced by misguided opinions, we should regularly ask the child the following key questions:

- *Are you enjoying it?*
- *Are you learning?*
- *Do you feel like you are improving?*
- *When you play do you find it easy or difficult?*
- *Do you feel under any pressure to play well?*

The answers to these questions will undoubtedly offer us important information regarding whether a young player is experiencing the appropriate level of challenge. Professor Lenny Wiersma of California State University uses a useful analogy to articulate this point: **"One reason kids love video games so much is that they can each pick their own level of challenge."**[93]

When we get this balance right, players' confidence levels undoubtedly flourish. This in turn elevates a desire to be more engaged in games, which means more touches on the ball and decision making opportunities. Researchers Professor James Mandingo and Dr. Nicholas Holt provide us with an insightful view on this issue in their investigation into motivation in youth sports:

> When individuals take part in activities that challenge them in a positive way (i.e., the activity is neither too hard nor too easy relative to their skill level) their competence is enhanced. This enhanced competence leads to individuals feeling intrinsically motivated to participate.[94]

Of course if players begin to demonstrate higher levels of capability, then we can look at increasing the challenge accordingly. **The key is recognizing the need for sensible progression, not going from level 3 to level 9 and skipping the levels in between,** which was clearly the case for Sally in this scenario.

Scenario 2: Players demonstrating advanced capabilities in need of an increased challenge

*Liam, 11 years of age, loves soccer and has had a ball at his feet since he could walk. Although **physically** small for his age, he has great balance, co-ordination, and speed, and also shows outstanding **technical** skills while playing for his U11 club team. From a psychological perspective Liam has also demonstrated resilience in the face of adversity and that he is emotionally stable. After watching him dribble past opponents and scoring goals with ease, the coach decides it would be good for him to play up at the U12 age group. (Note: 'playing up' is a term used in youth soccer when players participate in an older age category.)*

When players demonstrate advanced capabilities there are two common ways that clubs and coaches deal with this situation:

1. Just having him play up with no developmental consideration - From various perspectives this player may be suited to play up. However, we have seen numerous players over the years getting pushed into this scenario and sometimes playing 2 or 3 age groups up without considering these critical questions:

- *Does the player want to play up?*

- *Is the player physically capable of playing with and against older players?*

- *Can the player fit in socially?*

- *Is the player emotionally capable of playing with an older age group?*

- *Does the player possess the appropriate game understanding to play at a higher level of competition?*

2. Holding players back and not allowing them the appropriate challenge which their progressive needs require - Often due to short term objectives, convenience, and political reasons, clubs and coaches commonly implement policies that players must only play in their age group.

For example, many coaches are strongly opposed to releasing exceptional players from their team as these players have far too much influence on the game when playing in their own age group and can help clubs and coaches obtain trophies and produce winning performances they desperately seek. U.S. youth soccer director Sam Snow offers some stern words of warning against this approach: **"Under no circumstances should coaches exploit or hold players back in the misplaced quest for team building and winning championships."**[95]

During our research we spoke with various coaches and directors working with different clubs throughout the U.S. who affirmed that playing players up causes significant problems with parents in their organization; often causing many other parents to demand the same opportunity for their child, *frequently due to the misguided belief we discussed earlier that pushing players and offering them tougher challenges and levels of competition is good for **everyone***. Therefore, regardless of whether a young player needs this for their development, some clubs and coaches deny players of this opportunity and in some cases implement rules stopping individual players from playing up simply because of the problems it causes.

But clearly, any club or organization claiming that their primary focus is on player development cannot allow the opinions and demands of parents to influence their decisions or take a form of action which fails to meet the best interests of the players' development. However, many clubs become primarily concerned about keeping parents happy meaning their self-proclaiming stance on development is yet another contradiction we see made time and time again.

When a young player is displaying advanced capabilities and finding a certain level of challenge far too easy, simply holding them back and not offering them an alternative can be damaging in both the short and long-term.

First, in the short-term, due to the lack of challenge players can become disinterested, and begin to lose their passion for the game. In the long-term, players who are held back and who do not receive the appropriate levels of challenge today can fail to progress and unlock their potential. An easy way to look at this is again by using an academic analogy. If a student demonstrates advanced reading capability at 11 years of age, would we subject them to reading only the same books as the rest of the class just to keep the other students' parents happy, or would we allow the youngster in question to read more stimulating material? Again, U.S. youth soccer director Sam Snow shares his opinion on this matter:

> Rules restricting an individual player's option to play at the appropriate competitive level are in effect impeding that player's opportunity for growth. For development to occur, all players must be exposed to levels of competition commensurate with their skills and must be challenged constantly in matches in order to aspire to higher levels of play and maintain their interest in and passion for the game.[96]

We must reiterate, **enjoyment and learning are the foremost objectives when we are working with young players**. With this in mind and taking readiness into account, we can see that offering Liam an increased level of challenge to continue with his development as a player is a step in the right direction. Again, he displays excellent **technical and psychological capabilities,** but his small physical size is certainly a factor and must be given consideration.

When faced with this scenario, we must explore all available options and resources. But before we can do that we must ensure that:

A. **Clubs are not concerned about pleasing parents.**

B. **They truly focus only on what they believe is best for each players' individual development.**

C. **All the coaches in the club share this same vision.**

So, with these ideals in place, we can now look at how we can help Liam. First, soccer clubs often have teams in each chronological age group, so the ability to facilitate the needs of players frequently exists. For example, if Liam's U11 coach is working in harmony with the U12 coach in his club, they can communicate and create the following outcome:

U11 Coach: *"Liam has been doing very well lately and I believe he needs an increased challenge to suit his progressive needs and maintain his passion for the sport. However, I am a little hesitant to ask you simply to throw him into any U12 game, as his physical size could put him at risk. Are there any upcoming situations you feel may be beneficial for him?"*

U12 Coach: *"Well, I currently have the boys playing in the Red League where it is physically demanding and competitive. But my friend is the coach of the Rovers team which we play in a couple of weeks, and his team is very technically skilled. We often work together so both teams can work on developmental aspects during the game. I think this may be a perfect opportunity for Liam!"*

*Even though the U11's and U12's play at the same time, Liam's U11 coach believes that it would be in **Liam's best interests** to have him go and play in this game with the U12's. Therefore, after training, he approaches Liam and tells him,*

*You have been doing very well, and I believe that it would be very good for you to experience a little more of a challenge. With that said, **and it's totally your decision**, would you like the opportunity to play with the U12 team in an upcoming game? It would be once in a while and it would only be when we think it is going to be good for your development as there are some big strong boys in that league who could be physically too much for you right now, and for that reason we don't want you playing there every week. But we feel this game will be a good situation. What do you think?*

Liam, excited and filled with confidence, decides that although he would miss playing with his friends, he would love the opportunity. So he plays up with the U12 team and enjoys the challenge and the experience.

This was an excellent solution allowing this young player to experience a level of challenge that would positively impact his development and passion for the game. A key point in this scenario was that the player was **given the choice**. Again, when it comes to the subject of challenge, the majority of young players will enjoy their experience and activities much more if they have some influence in deciding which level of challenge they encounter.

Since some clubs may not always have an older team for a young player to play up with, we must consider how we can provide them with an increased challenge during games in their own age group. A valuable tool we can utilize without changing the opposition or environment is by setting **individual functional challenges** during games. Depending on which position the player is in, we can ask the player to attempt a specific task related to that role. For example, if the player is playing right midfield we could ask, "How many times can you dribble past a player and find a team mate in the box?" If they are playing central defense or midfield, we could ask the player to receive the ball from the right side of the field and switch it to the left, and vice versa, when they feel it is the appropriate moment to do so. If they are playing fullback (right or left side defense), we can ask them to get forward and overlap when they think the time is right.

The great value of implementing these individual functional challenges is that it allows coaches to set suitable tasks for players of all ability levels, as even with the less advanced players we can ask them to attempt basic fundamental concepts. However, the true magnitude of this method can be observed with those players who are facing inferior opposition and when the challenge of the game itself is too easy.

Scenario 3: Playing the whole team up

*The coach of a U11 team made up of 14 players of **various levels of ability** decides to play his team up in age group in the U12 league, believing that the challenge is going to make his team better. But out of the fourteen players, the level of challenge at the U12 age group is only beneficial for four players as they possess sound game understanding and are 'ready' from a technical, physical, and psychological perspective. For seven of the players, playing at the U11 age group has been a great experience developmentally which they have also enjoyed. However, the level of challenge they will face at the U12 age group will be overwhelming since they do not possess the necessary attributes. Finally, for the remaining three players, facing the challenges at the U12 age group will likely have a destructive impact on their immediate experiences and development, since they even found it difficult playing in the U11 league.*

This scenario demonstrates a common decision made by many clubs and coaches. And while there are similarities, we must point out that this is a different state of affairs than the circumstances in **scenario 2**, as this is going to impact **14 players** and not just **one individual**. Therefore, we must consider the ramifications of this approach.

First, as was the case for Liam in Scenario 2, four players can benefit from the additional challenge of playing up. Although, we must consider that their situation will not be as healthy as Liam's, because he was able to play with older more advanced players, whereas these four players would be playing up with teammates who are **not equipped to play at this level**. And as we mentioned earlier this can lead to the advanced players becoming frustrated with their less capable teammates who are not ready for the demands of higher levels of competition.

But playing the whole team up when only four players are ready to face a higher level of challenge **makes no sense from a developmental standpoint.** As we have observed, this scenario will frequently result in negative consequences for the other players who are not ready. We must consider the thoughts provided by authors Robert Dilts and Deborah Bacon Dilts in their article "Coaching at the Identity Level", who state, "I am not going to treat you all the same. You are different from each other in height, weight, background, intelligence, talent, and many other ways. For that reason **each one of you deserves individual treatment that is best for you.**"[97]

The coach in this scenario evidently fails to embrace this principle. First of all, we have three players who found it difficult playing even in the U11 league, and now they are going to have to face the overwhelming demands of the U12 level. Additionally, the same move was decided on for seven players who were enjoying their experiences and developing effectively playing in their own age group. These players will now be pushed into a situation which will be less enjoyable and effective for their continued progress, a mirror image of what was thrust upon Sally in **scenario 1,** and as the ramifications are the same we have no need to discuss them again here.

Again, the reasoning for this decision is often based on interests **other than what is best for each individual's development.** For example, the main driver for playing the team up is that many coaches believe it will magically lead to future **team success** when their team plays back down at their 'real' age group due to consistently facing the challenge of playing against older teams. This is confirmed by some of the responses that we have encountered over the years when asking coaches the rationale behind their decision:

- *"We have a tournament coming up in a couple of months and playing against these older teams is great preparation!"*

- *"Well, although they are struggling now, they will soon be a force to be reckoned with!"*

- *"I want my players to be more aggressive! Playing up against bigger stronger players is going to toughen them up!"*

As we outlined earlier, many coaches and parents fail to question the theories they hear regarding challenging players in this manner, and consequently, they end up believing misguided notions that are not supported by empirical evidence. Habitually, they just hear others making erroneous statements and robotically repeat them as though it is factual information. As is often the case, not enough thought goes into whether this situation is going to be good for **every player**.

But we must also acknowledge that some coaches and parents have other reasons for having young players play up. For example, due to being ego-involved and not wanting to be perceived as incompetent, some coaches play their team up so if they lose they have the excuse of saying, *"Well, it's to be expected, our players are so much younger".* This theory is supported by the fact that throughout our coaching experiences we have encountered numerous coaches **voluntarily inform us after a defeat** that their team contains younger players who are playing up. Additionally, many parents take great pleasure from announcing to other parents that their child doesn't play in their own age group because they are far too advanced and need the challenge of playing against older players.

However, any coach or parent encouraging playing up without considering the key questions that we outlined at the beginning of **scenario 2** and/or merely because their objective is to prepare the team for future success is completely misguided in their approach if they believe they are doing what is best for player development. We have observed numerous cases over the years where self-proclaimed leading clubs play entire teams up without caring that some of the players are not ready and would clearly benefit far more from playing in an age appropriate situation. Once again, these clubs still espouse that they are focusing on everyone's individual development.

But we must accept that due to the conventional mindset in youth soccer, and specifically how team success is constantly placed before each individual's development, providing young players with the appropriate level of challenge can be difficult. If player development is the primary focus, playing this whole team up is not the path to take. Instead, what should happen in this scenario is the following:

- *The four advanced players should play up at U12 with a different group of players.*

- *The seven players who were developing well at the U11 level should remain in this environment.*

- *The three weaker players should be provided with an easier and more comfortable playing situation.*

This approach would likely spark strong opposition from many coaches and parents who would protest, ***"We have great team chemistry!"*** or ***"These guys have played together for 3 years - you can't split them up now!".*** We have to appreciate that healthy relationships play a major role in youth soccer, and as we highlight in chapter one, studies suggest that being with and making friends are one of the main reasons children participate in sport. However, what many coaches and parents fail to value and emphasize is that young players can meet new friends and develop healthy relationships in new settings. We have observed there is a higher likelihood that friendships and experiences will be enriched due to players sharing similar levels of ability and progressive needs.

When merely placing young players on a team and keeping them together regardless of their capabilities, we must accept the fact that **individual**

development has taken a back seat. Again, just as we outlined in each scenario, the challenges young players face should be appropriate to their progressive needs. They should be like their shoes: Fit perfectly and feel comfortable. This will afford players the opportunity to practice important developmental aspects during the most critical period of their experiences.

Chapter Seven

Tournaments

"Precisely because we are so immersed in it, competition can easily escape our notice. A fish does not reflect on the nature of the water, he cannot imagine its absence, so cannot consider its presence."[98]

Walker Percy - American Author

When originally introduced, soccer tournaments in the U.S. merely offered the opportunity for healthy interaction between teams and a way to celebrate the game during a time when soccer was less popular. With far fewer teams around, players were required to travel from their cities and towns just to find other teams to play against. Then as the game of soccer developed, tournaments moved onto their next phase serving as excellent fundraising opportunities for many clubs.

But today these ideals are a distant memory, and tournaments have transformed dramatically with their current nature representing an ultra-competitive, high pressure, frenzied environment, magnifying all the negative aspects in youth soccer highlighted in this book. Consequently, the subject of tournaments has arguably become one of the most contentious issues in U.S. youth soccer as significant amounts of research demonstrates there will be harmful ramifications for young players subjected to consistent tournament exposure. Therefore, it is not surprising that there are 55 state Technical Directors in the U.S. responsible for the development and growth of young players who express **significant concern** regarding the current nature of tournaments.[99]

These views are substantiated by researcher Dr. J. Martin in his discussion of tournaments and player development in youth soccer: **"Tournaments are killing soccer in this country. Young players can't learn how to play in these types of situations. Everything about these tournaments is bad for the development of American soccer players."**[100] In addition, leading professional soccer coach Sigi

Schmid stresses the current format of youth soccer tournaments in the U.S **retards rather than enhances player development.**[101]

But despite the concerns raised by development experts and leading directors, not only do many clubs, coaches, and parents unwaveringly demonstrate **a strong desire to constantly push young players** into these highly frenetic and stressful events; incredibly, many repeatedly travel hundreds of miles to other states spending vast amounts of time, effort, and money attending them. However, as we discussed in the introduction to this book, Bobby Howe, the former Director of Coaching for the United States Soccer Federation affirms, **"There is no need for players under the age of 13 to play out of state."**[102]

This crazed obsession referred to as **'tournamentitis'** by U.S. youth soccer director Sam Snow creates a significant amount of work for those attempting to take a positive developmental approach.[103] For many years, we have had to explain why we do not advocate traveling to tournaments during the early stages of young players' development. Often, parents in our program have become inquisitive because individuals from other organizations, who have no insight into the negative repercussions of tournaments or what researchers and leading figures in youth soccer are trying to convey, simply declare, *"You guys don't go to tournaments? Well…. You're going to miss out!"* Because of such scenarios, we have to consistently reassure parents by describing the problems and damage these tournaments cause.

But before we emphasize what is actually happening at these tournaments, we feel it is beneficial to briefly highlight some of the reasons why coaches and parents persistently drag young players all over the nation to attend these meaningless events.

First, clubs and coaches trying to obtain early team success is undoubtedly the primary driver as to why so many relentlessly travel significant distances to these tournaments. Even with the **youngest age groups**, these clubs and coaches boast about tournament wins at every opportunity, with many plastering pictures all over their websites of young players holding trophies while offering a detailed account about how nine year old Johnny scored the winner in overtime after playing in four consecutive games in the blistering summer heat! We only have to consider the views of our own U.S. Technical Director Claudio Reyna to shed some light on how ridiculous this state of affairs really is during the early stages of the players' development:

> For me, it's irrelevant if coaches win state cups, regional cups, and national cups. How many trophies they have in their cabinet isn't important. **It's about the kids, it's not about you.** We care about how many players you develop rather than how many trophies you win.[104]

Additionally, many coaches and parents falsely assume that traveling all over and pushing players into the highly competitive games found at these tournaments is an essential requirement that will **'magically'** elevate **all players** to great things in the future regardless of whether an individual is ready for the level of challenge.

We must consider that the nature of competition consistently found at these tournaments was never designed for the players' best interests. As long-term athlete development experts Dr. Istvan Balyi and Richard Way assert:

> Competition is a critical issue in all sports, especially team sports. Unfortunately, the system of competition in many sports was never properly designed; it simply 'evolved' on an improvised basis without consideration for the sport science of athlete development. Now many competition schedules are considered part of the tradition of certain sports, and these habitual patterns are passionately adhered to. "This is the way we have always done it!"[105]

Therefore, many coaches and parents suffer from 'tournamentitis' because they simply repeat tradition and emulate what other clubs, coaches, and parents do without considering whether this course of action is actually beneficial for their child.

We must also acknowledge that many parents constantly thrust their children into tournaments because the experience **offers them personal utility**. Falling into the 'reverse dependency trap,' many parents, looking to fulfill their own curiosity, push their children into these negative environments simply because they want to see how they compete and compare with the 'best' players and teams around. But again, being concerned about how your child measures against 9, 10, or 11 year old children from another state is a waste of time because (as we discussed in 'Talent Identification and Potential') significant variances in growth and development will take place between players; so how your child compares now will most likely be completely different in the near future anyway. However, **desperate for another 'fix'**, many parents march on as they are driven by an insatiable appetite for the temporary gratification coming from their child's and their team's performing well while picking up another trivial medal on the 'big stage'.

The **social aspect** is also appealing to many parents who love nothing more than sitting around the tables of hotel lobbies with drinks and snacks, comparing players, discussing what tactics should be employed in the forthcoming game, and deciding upon which tournament they are going to attend next! Then with no substantial evidence whatsoever about whether playing in these tournaments is actually beneficial for their child's development, these parents go back home and boast to their friends and colleagues how far they traveled at the weekend, robotically repeating and emphasizing how great this tournament experience was for their child.

After briefly looking at some of these reasons, it is no wonder why our Director of Coaching for U.S. Youth Soccer, Sam Snow, claims, **"Often teams participate in tournaments for poor soccer reasons or no soccer reason at all!"**[106]

As we discussed earlier in the book, during the players' formative years games must be consistently utilized primarily from a learning perspective while offering challenges that meet their progressive needs. But this is extremely difficult to achieve at these tournaments because many coaches often have limited or zero information about their opponents. Therefore, they cannot evaluate the level of challenge that their players are going to be exposed to. Consequently, players are frequently faced with situations they are not ready for and are not offered the chance to use these games as crucial learning experiences.

But let's assume that a coach has a healthy philosophy toward youth development and takes a group of young players to a tournament with the primary objective of using the games as learning opportunities. Additionally, let's suppose the coach also has some insight about the level of challenge that his players will encounter due to his knowledge of the opposition's players. Even with these two positive factors in place, providing a positive setting for players is extremely difficult as the current nature of tournaments **significantly amplifies** all the negative aspects of youth soccer we discuss in this book, which are clearly detrimental for the young players' experiences and development.

For example, in the chapter 'Sideline Instruction' we discuss how young players must be offered the freedom to make their own decisions and solve their own problems with minimal intervention. However, the detrimental impact coaches and parents have on young players when they bombard them with **directions from the sideline is considerably magnified at these tournaments.** Often, coaches and parents simply **hijack** the games, constantly stifling the players' opportunities to make their own decisions, experiment, and implement imaginative skills. This is especially the case as the climax of the tournament draws near and the sound levels from the sideline increase significantly as numerous coaches and dozens of parents simultaneously attempt to convey their own personal message to the players.

In this setting, many parents seemingly **transform in character** displaying irrational behavior while losing control of their emotions. This repeatedly occurs in the presence of young people when parents should be creating a healthy and positive environment. In their study investigating parental involvement in youth sport Dr. Chris Harwood and Camilla Knight state, **"While parents are required to provide their children with sufficient support, they are sometimes unable to cope with the emotional demands that they face themselves."**[107]

In chapter three, we discuss how mistakes should be utilized positively to facilitate the players' understanding of the game and develop confidence. But as we also detailed, many coaches and parents deal with players' mistakes very negatively, and **there is no better arena for this behavior to raise its ugly face than at these tournaments**. Allowing their emotions to spiral out of control, coaches and parents consistently yell scathing and disapproving comments at players, which leave many youngsters feeling dejected, embarrassed, anxious, and as though they have travelled all that distance solely to **satisfy the coaches' and parents' desires.**

When we analyze the way coaches and parents behave at these tournaments, this alone demonstrates why they have severe consequences for young players. Professor Douglas Abrams, from the University of Missouri, concisely explains how such inappropriate behavior found at these tournaments can impact young players:

> **Screaming, ridicule and other adult-imposed pressures do nothing to toughen child athletes, hone their skills, or enhance their competitive spirit.** Indeed, the pressure often backfires by inducing debilitating fear of failure, which inhibits performance and leads some children to seek comfort on the sidelines by feigning or over-exaggerating injury or by quitting altogether.[108]

At these tournaments many young players who are perceived as weaker members of the roster receive limited amounts of playing time. We have often asked from a developmental perspective why parents would ever haul their child hundreds of miles to spend the majority of their time on the bench. In the chapter four, we highlight the importance of offering all young players equal amounts of playing time. However, **these tournaments offer the perfect setting for coaches to deprive players of playing opportunities due to their ceaseless drive for tournament success.**

Another issue which makes no sense from a developmental viewpoint is how the more advanced players are utilized inappropriately at these tournaments.

Frequently exploited, many of the 'better' players are relentlessly pushed game after game, as winning is the main objective for many coaches and parents. And due to the demanding tournament schedule, **the players' wellbeing simply takes a back seat**, when many young players play **excessive amounts** in a highly competitive environment without sufficient time to recover.

In soccer, the risk of players suffering impact injuries and getting hurt is always a factor. However, a major concern for players participating in these tournaments is the prevalence of 'overuse injury,' which alarmingly **accounts for up to 50% of injuries in youth sport.**[109] According to pediatric expert Dr. Joel Brenner, an overuse injury is damage to a bone, muscle, or tendon that has been subjected to repetitive stress without sufficient time to recover or heal.[110] With young players often required to perform in three or four games within a 48 hour period, such figures are hardly surprising, especially when one considers how these games are often highly competitive and demanding, and require incredible effort from players. Bobby Howe, former Director of Coaching for the U.S. Soccer Federation, expresses how the importance of recovery time is often overlooked at tournaments: "Rest and regeneration are as vital to overall preparation as training. Yet, **many tournament organizers neglect this very important component**".[111]

Research carried out by Lille Olympique Sporting Club sports scientist Dr. Gregory Dupont and his colleagues investigating how the effects of a congested soccer schedule on injury rate of elite soccer players puts these injury concerns into perspective. They established that when elite athletes played in two games **in a week** rather than just one they were six times more likely to suffer injury.[112] Again, we must remember that these are professional players receiving leading medical and sports science support, and insufficient recovery time between games over a much longer period was a crucial factor even for them.

The crucial point is that constantly pushing young players in overly demanding tournament schedules with little regard for their wellbeing significantly increases the chance of their suffering an injury. Dr. Bradley Abrahamson a specialist in sports medicine succinctly captures the increased injury risk witnessed at these tournaments by claiming that **"Tournament play**

in youth soccer is a common precursor to a medical visit", a risk significantly magnified for the clubs that choose to expose their young players' to numerous tournaments throughout the course of a season. [113]

Additionally, because of the overly demanding schedule witnessed at these tournaments, the players' nutritional requirements take on added importance. It is not our intention in this book to provide a detailed scientific analysis of the nutritional necessities of a youth soccer tournament; however, we must consider that even when young players participate in just one game, a main nutritional concern relates to the way glycogen levels *(carbohydrate stored in the muscles)* become severely depleted towards the end of the game. Yet at these tournaments as players are often asked to play in 3 or 4 games in quick succession it is very difficult to maintain adequate fuel levels and players will suffer from a number of perspectives.

For example, players whose glycogen levels start to deplete will often experience signs of fatigue, generally suffer a considerable dip in their performance level, and begin to lose concentration, all of which places them at higher risk of incurring an injury. A number of researchers and nutritional experts express concerns about the over demanding tournament schedules and the problems they present from a nutritional standpoint. For instance, Nanna Meyer, Assistant Professor at the University of Colorado, affirms:

> Tournaments offer a unique nutritional challenge for soccer players. Because multiple games are played in one day, little time is available for athletes to recover and properly replace fuel stores. However, not replacing these stores will result in decreased performance and faster fatigue, which compromises a soccer player's skill, speed, and concentration and possibly increases the risk of injury.[114]

An important point we must make is that the nutritional problems are often exacerbated by the fact that many of these tournaments offer inappropriate food options for young players to re-fuel in between their frequently grueling schedules. Sports nutritionist Michele Macedonio points out that concession stands at tournaments offer limited selections, often with many high-fat foods.[115] **Burgers, hot-dogs, doughnuts, sodas, and pizzas are commonplace at these tournaments**, but many coaches and parents allow youngsters to regularly consume these terrible food choices, yet they still demand game winning performances!

Additionally, as these tournaments often take place during hot seasons, the degree of dehydration and its associated dangers increase significantly. In their study investigating fluid consumption and sweat rates in youth soccer players, Professor Matthew Ganio and colleagues point out that young soccer players can potentially lose up to 0.6 to 1 liter of water per hour of soccer activity in hot environments, which provides us with an idea of the type of fluid loss players will experience if they are playing in a number of games in the same day in these types of conditions.[116]

The American Dietetic Association states that particular attention needs to be paid to young players' fluid losses, as children produce more heat in comparison to adults during exercise. Furthermore, youngsters have lower sweating rates than adults, so it takes them longer to become accustomed to hot weather.[117] Players who begin to become dehydrated will fatigue quicker, lose concentration, and their performance levels will suffer adverse effects. Additionally, they will often experience more serious symptoms in the form of headaches, nausea, dizziness, and consistent muscle cramps, and if left unnoticed, **dehydration can rapidly lead to heat exhaustion and even heat stroke, which can result in deadly consequences if not treated appropriately.**

During our research, we witnessed many tournaments taking place in excessively high temperatures. In one of the more notable examples, we observed how a self-proclaimed leading club subjected their U9 boys to a tournament in Pennsylvania over the weekend of July 7th and 8th in 2012. On this dangerously hot weekend which prompted safety warnings to the general public, these young players had to endure three games, with one game played at 3:15pm on July 7th **when the temperature peaked at 104F.**

Interestingly, in guidelines related to heat stress in young children, the American Academy of Pediatrics recommends that when temperatures exceed

85F it is a critical level which calls for organizations and coaches to **"cancel all athletic activities"**.[118] Again, in many states these tournaments take place during the hotter periods of the year, so we are well aware that tournament organizers will bypass this recommendation and run events in temperatures ranging from the upper 80's to the lower 90's, regardless of other climatic considerations such as humidity and those outlined by the WBGT index. However, when and where is the line going to be drawn? Common sense tells us that 8 and 9 year olds do not need to be playing in 104F. This is not a healthy situation. **Why then would any club espousing player development as their primary objective expose young players to such extreme conditions?**

Either clubs are not aware that such recommendations or dangers exist, or they choose to ignore this risk associated with pushing young players into extreme environmental settings. Evidence strongly suggests that it is the latter, as many of these clubs again have documents and articles linked to their website regarding health and safety issues of this precise nature. As is often the case, many coaches and parents simply want the **'show to go on'** regardless of the conditions and ramifications, especially if they have travelled a significant distance to attend a particular tournament.

Finally, we have observed many times how the field dimensions at tournaments also make no sense from a player development perspective. Young players are often asked to perform not only in multiple games in hot temperatures over one weekend, but are also asked to do it on huge fields designed for adults and players in their late teens. But time and time again, many coaches and parents bypass this critical concern simply believing that this is another stern challenge that will miraculously take players to the next level.

Indisputably, the problems and ramifications for young players participating at these tournaments completely outweigh any of the reasons that clubs, coaches, and parents use to justify attending them. The fact that leading figures in youth soccer, developmental experts, and researchers strongly oppose young players being constantly thrust into these tournaments speaks for itself. Therefore, the fact that so many clubs, organizations, and coaches promote and encourage parents and players to attend such events **is a huge problem that must be addressed.**

Note: There are tournaments where there are no recorded scores, standings, or winners' trophies at the younger age groups which have been labeled 'Festivals'. **This suggests that some tournament organizers recognize the need for change.** *But unfortunately, we have observed a number of these 'Festival' events, and although there were no scores or standings, the playing environment and tournament format was just as detrimental, and many coaches and parents were keeping score as they do in the traditional manner at these events.*

For example, during multiple games in a two day period, coaches and parents were yelling onto the field, giving constant instruction and offering typical negative responses when players made mistakes, when referees made a questionable decision, or their team gave up a goal; and remarkably, the **coaches emphasized the score to their players during and after the game, even though no scores were recorded!**

So although it seems that there are tournament organizers who want to make a positive difference by implementing these 'festivals', evidence suggests that they need to have **more conviction** *with their execution and that they must be steadfast when addressing coaches' and parents' behavior in order to pull away from the conventional tournament environment.*

An Alternative Approach

To find a better solution than subjecting young players to tournaments, we asked numerous parents and players involved in youth soccer why they enjoyed going to these events. These were the top three responses:

1. **The enjoyment of playing against teams from other areas who they have never played against before.**

2. ***The social aspect: Players and adults enjoy being with their friends and spending the night in a hotel.***

3. ***Parents like to see how their kids compare to players from other areas.***

The first point we need to recognize is that all of these needs can be achieved without jumping on the tournament bandwagon with young players. **But we must reiterate that response number 3. should never be a consideration during the early stages of development anyway.** With some thought and creativity, we can certainly make a positive difference and change the outlook on the tournament landscape.

In order to demonstrate this point here is the first solution:

A group of U10 girls, their parents, and coach would enjoy playing against teams they have never played before. They would also enjoy the experience of staying in a hotel overnight during the weekend. Therefore, the coach identifies a few cities a couple of hours away, and looks up the local soccer clubs in those areas. He then sends emails to various coaches and club administrators explaining that his team is looking at setting up a couple of friendly games while visiting their city. He receives some responses and after a couple of conversations and emails sets up two games, one on Saturday and one on Sunday.

Everyone enjoyed the trip, and importantly the games were fun and educational as all players received equal amounts of playing time while playing against teams they have never seen before. Furthermore, as winning took a back seat, the game environment was much healthier than what they experienced previously at tournaments. Finally, during their stay, they visited a local attraction and the coach was able to *network and create new positive relationships that could be utilized effectively for the **players' best interests** in the future.*

Over the years we have frequently worked with a number of organizations in this fashion. This is a simple and productive concept to implement requiring limited administrative work and demands. And since we share similar philosophies, we are able to coordinate these events so that **all players** benefit from the experience and ensure the playing environment is a positive one where learning and enjoyment are the main priority.

Another beneficial tool that we have implemented instead of the conventional tournament is to set up our own internal activities. Over the years we have set up numerous events where we divide up the young players in our training program based on their developmental needs and create teams like USA, England, Brazil, and Spain to make it more fun. The teams play in a round robin format and follow an appropriate schedule of no more than three 25 minute small-sided games in a 4 v 4 or 5 v 5 format. Importantly, the elimination factor is taken out of the equation and there are no trophies to be won, as again this distracts players from learning. Karl Dewaizen, a leading youth soccer coach who has spoken out over the detrimental impact of tournaments for a number of years, confirms how positive this alternative approach is: "***With no elimination and no ultimate winner, stress is reduced. Players, coaches, and spectators can focus on the enjoyment of soccer – and the acquisition of skills – without worrying about results.***"[119]

Offering players the chance to play in these small-sided games enhances their opportunity to work with the ball and encounter an abundance of problem-solving situations, something we will discuss in more detail in the following chapter 'Training Considerations'. When we organize these events we always reiterate to the players and parents that we are here to try things, be creative, and have fun. Many parents thank us for setting these situations up, understanding their value and observing how happy their children are when they participate in them.

The critical point is that clubs and organizations can provide young players with excellent playing opportunities and enjoyable social aspects by implementing alternative methods and ideas. Instead of promoting conventional tournaments, clubs and organizations must make an effort to raise awareness of the problems so that coaches and parents understand why they should not be subjecting their young children to these detrimental events. However, as is frequently the case, **it is often too late when parents realize that the damage has been done and the years of unnecessary tournament participation has taken its toll.**

Chapter Eight

Training Considerations

"Without inspiration the best powers of the mind remain dormant. There is a fuel in us which needs to be ignited with sparks."[120]

Johann Gottfried Von Herder

As coaches and parents, the training system which we choose to utilize in the development of young players can hugely impact their future in the sport. Therefore, deciding on which training methods and philosophy we want for young players is an important decision that should not be underestimated or made without any investigation. Fortunately, the opportunity to reflect upon our decisions and actions is forever present, and we must always accept that just like young players we are always learning, and the need to embrace new concepts and a willingness to change is crucial.

Throughout our research we had a number of insightful discussions with elite coaches and youth development experts in different countries throughout Europe and North America who offered us some excellent feedback and ideas in relation to our own training curriculum. During our stay in the U.K., we observed training sessions at various youth academies throughout England. Speaking with elite coaches in these environments further confirmed our philosophy on player development and the necessity to focus on everyone's individual needs.

We also observed numerous training sessions in the U.S. involving recreational teams, travel teams, and organizations who charge fees for their coaching services. After a few sessions, we began to identify some common themes taking place which made no sense from a player development perspective. Furthermore, many aspects of the training seemed geared towards team concepts and short-term success, which contradicted the opinions of leading experts we spoke to relating to what they believe to be beneficial. Also, these themes that we observed are strongly opposed by many leading figures in U.S. youth soccer, whose primary objectives are to educate coaches, parents, and players, encourage more people to remain in the sport, and facilitate the development of elite players.

We will now highlight our observations and investigate the effects they have on young players' development.

Observation 1: Players were inactive for long periods of time

A very common observation that we consistently made during our research was **players standing still for prolonged periods** of time during training practices. There were two primary reasons why this occurred:

1. *During drills many players were inactive and stood waiting in line for their turn.*

2. *Coaches constantly stopped play to spend significant amounts of time talking and relaying information.*

We will now look at each one separately.

First, setting up drills with long lines is a very common mistake many coaches make in youth soccer. We observed many different passing, shooting, attacking, and defending drills where young players were disengaged for excessively long spells. The most notable example of this was when coaches ran shooting drills. For instance, in one particular session we observed a coach taking **14 players** through a shooting exercise which lasted approximately 25 minutes. In this drill, each player took turns shooting on goal after the coach served them with a ball. Then after taking a shot each player would return to the back of the line and wait their turn.

While watching this drill, we began to time how long this process took from one girl's individual perspective. Here is what we observed:

*We started the clock when she took her 1st shot. It then took **2 minutes** and **21 seconds** for her to take her 2nd shot. She then waited **2 minutes** **34 seconds** to take her 3rd shot, and **6 minutes** and **14 seconds** to take her 4th shot (this additional time was largely due to the coach stopping the drill to tell the players to stop misbehaving in line).*

*Therefore, this player had a total of **4 shots** in **11 minutes** and **9 seconds**.*

It would be fair to say that in this scenario this young player actually worked on her technical development for approximately **10 seconds in total**, which was the accumulative time required for her to take a couple of quick steps and a shot on four occasions. The rest of the 11 minutes was primarily spent getting back in line and being inactive as she waited for her next chance.

So, how much technical development and progress is this player going to make in this scenario? Well, the answer is not very much!

One does not need a Ph.D. in youth soccer development to realize that many young players will have limited technical capabilities if they are consistently subjected to scenarios such as these. It is easy to see that coaches who implement these types of drills are clearly **squandering valuable amounts of training time** that must be dedicated to developing good physical literacy and technique. We will look at this process in more detail in the second half of this chapter.

In spite of this, many coaches conventionally set up drill after drill *(often throughout the entire practice),* and consider it logical and standard practice for players to be stood in line for unnecessarily large amounts of time, a reason why it happens so often at all levels of youth soccer. As Mike Woitalla and U.S. Youth Soccer Technical Director Claudio Reyna point out, **"Players don't want to stand around in line behind cones, waiting for their turn to do something. They just need to get out and get as many touches of the ball as they can."**[121]

Players stood in line for long spells during practice.
A common mistake many coaches make in U.S. Youth Soccer.

Obviously, Reyna highlights this simple point because the majority of players find it extremely boring. And if young players are uninterested in the training exercises presented to them it will reduce their passion to be there. In the shooting scenario just discussed, the coach felt the need to stop the drill to tell his players to stop misbehaving in line. But did he at any point consider why they were becoming agitated and unsettled in the first place? Did he even question whether this exercise was enjoyable for the players?

Another common occurrence we observed causing players to be inactive for long periods was when coaches felt the need to **regularly stop and talk for lengthy periods of the practice**. Of course, choosing moments to inject key points and make inspiring comments can certainly help young players' development and motivation levels, and this is a skill that often comes with experience. But on many occasions we observed coaches stopping practices extensively and offering young players instructions at every opportunity, frequently overloading them with information. Additionally, many coaches seemed too eager to rectify every mistake, causing them to continually stop activity while jumping from one tactical topic to the next. The detrimental impact of this approach is well known by a number of elite coaches and developmental experts. For example, in their investigation of the training activities utilized by youth soccer coaches, Dr. Paul Ford of Liverpool John Moores University in England and colleagues emphasize that:

> Although the provision of instruction and management is an essential component of the coaching process, recent empirical work has highlighted the **dangers involved in being overly prescriptive and in using these behaviors too frequently during practice.** At some stage learners have to perform on their own without direct guidance and instruction from coaches. Consequently, the challenge for coaches is to provide the least amount of instruction possible regardless of the athlete's age or skill.[122]

As we discussed in the chapter 'Sideline Instruction', many coaches believe that it is their responsibility to constantly direct and tell players what to do. But unlike in organized games, during training coaches have the ability to halt everything at any moment they choose; and unfortunately many coaches abuse this privilege and deny young players the opportunity to 'get on with it' by stopping practice time and time again whenever they see a coaching moment.

Again, some coaches behave in this manner simply to boost their own egos, believing they will impress parents and various other onlookers who often perceive such behavior as excellent coaching practice. Interestingly, in a discussion with the president of a soccer academy in Central New York, he stressed the importance of his coaches consistently halting practice sessions **just to make coaching points to keep parents happy** as they were spending money for their child to be coached by their organization. Of course, if parents are paying fees for their child's education, then providing guidance at the right moments should be expected. However, if coaches are consistently stopping practice due to these misguided ulterior motives, then quite simply young players' best interests are taking a back seat to coaches' egos and/or financial gain. In this state of affairs, they are not taking the right approach from a developmental perspective. **They are in fact faking it and putting on a show.**

In our discussion with elite sports coach, Daniel Massaro, who has worked with world class athletes for a number of years, he substantiated that this scenario is a common one in youth sport by saying:

> Many coaches involved in youth sports are frequently overly concerned about how their coaching ability is being perceived by the parents and other people watching their sessions. But rather than being concerned about how parents perceive you as a coach, it is far more important to concentrate on how your players perceive the practice. It takes a clear focus and confidence in the coach to stick by their philosophy in such situations. It is very tempting to pander to the paying parents with short term strategies such as throwing out lots of information or promising rapid improvements if they do what you say. A coach doesn't know what the future holds and is no fortune teller, but it can be what reassures parents. Coaches are tempted to sell themselves in this way either motivated by business opportunity or for quick and easy rapport. It is this that also prevents the inexperienced coach from being able to set certain parental rules regarding watching sessions and interfering with coaching decisions. The experienced and confident coach will be able to include (or exclude) the parents in a supportive, constructive and nonintrusive way.

From our early days as youth players right through to the professional ranks, we have concluded that it is extremely frustrating having a game, exercise, or activity regularly stopped because the coach wants to make another coaching point during training. As former Republic of Ireland and Manchester United captain Roy Keane points out, **"one of the keys to a proper training session is not to have players hanging around."**[123] Bear in mind that Keane is speaking about training at the professional level of the game. So if he is making this suggestion for elite level players, it supports the contention that **young players** who should be enjoying their experiences and developing a passion for the game should not be subjected to listening to long coaching 'lectures' during training or made to stand in line for excessive amounts of time.

Observation 2: Valuable training time was utilized to work on team set-plays and concepts

As players get older and progress in the sport, it becomes more important to develop their understanding of team concepts such as formations and set-plays. Therefore, in the later stages of development, when players have the capability to execute and comprehend such concepts, utilizing higher percentages of training time to enhance and facilitate their understanding is essential if we want them to become effective soccer players.

However, utilizing crucial practice time to work on elaborate team concepts during young players' formative years and **before players have even laid a solid physical and technical foundation** makes no sense from a player development standpoint. To demonstrate this point here are two simple examples that we observed:

Example 1: One coach worked on the offside trap with a U10 team for over 45 minutes. During this time, his players were made to stand for long spells while he talked and told them what he needed them to do. Many players never touched the ball, and they looked as though they were not enjoying the practice.

Example 2: One coach dedicated the majority of his practice attempting to improve his U9 team's ability to score from corner kicks. In this specific scenario, one young player took every corner while his teammates (some playing offense and the rest playing defense) stood in the box waiting for his delivery. Although the boy taking the corners received an opportunity to work on crossing, the rest of the players in the box hardly touched the ball.

Implementing such training activities seems perfectly rational and natural to many coaches and parents. It also makes sense for many to utilize valuable training time working on what went wrong in the last game. The example where the coach worked on corner kicks with his young team demonstrates this point perfectly, as this coach informed us after his practice that his side had 13 corner kicks in their last game and didn't score from any of them!

But preparing the team for upcoming games or tournaments instead of focusing on young players' individual development is the conventional approach currently taken in U.S. youth soccer. This point is substantiated by many development experts and leading coaches in the game. In their study investigating effective talent development, Dr. Martindale and his colleagues confirm this when they state, **"The team is pushed far too much and the individual isn't. That's where team sports break down entirely. You've got to treat them all individually."**[124] Additionally, Ian Mulliner, former Director of Coaching for the Illinois Youth Soccer Association says:

> Having been involved in youth soccer for the past several years at the club, state and regional levels it is becoming apparent that **player development is taking a backseat to team performance**. It seems that the rush to create a successful team has become more important for coaches than allowing players to improve.[125]

Of course, spending a whole training session on corner kicks may very well increase the chances of victory at the weekend, but **if young players are stood still and hardly ever touching the ball how can we expect them to develop?** Unfortunately, many coaches and parents involved in youth soccer do not give this enough logical consideration.

This process in which coaches take short-cuts and place the focus on winning and immediate team success at the cost of the young players' development is referred to by athletic development experts Dr. Istvan Balyi and Ann Hamilton as **'Peaking by Friday'**.[126] But unfortunately, many coaches fail to understand that if they take this approach at the younger age groups, players will have to **sacrifice crucial development opportunities** vital to their progress in the sport.

When coaches choose this path with young players who have yet to lay a competent physical and technical foundation, they often fail to realize that not only are they denying young players the crucial time required to develop vital physical and technical attributes, but they are also putting the **'cart before the horse'**, as players are often incapable of executing the set-plays and various other team concepts effectively due to not yet having the capabilities. This precise point is made by arguably the best player ever to be produced by the U.S. All-time leading scorer for the men's national team, Landon Donovan states:

> "You can learn the tactical side of the game later. It's amazing to me that people put so much emphasis on trying to be tactical and worry about winning when it doesn't matter when you're 12 years old. We're going to have big, strong, fast players. We're Americans, we're athletes. But if we never learn at an early age to be good on the ball, then it's just useless.".[127]

Due to this logic not being appreciated, coaches unwaveringly march on with a misguided tactical approach which would be far more appropriate for college and professional athletes. Furthermore, what is remarkable is that many of these coaches frequently become frustrated and upset when their young players fail to display the cognitive processes or execute the technical skills required to give them the winning performance edge they so desperately seek.

We also witnessed coaches getting angry at players who displayed disinterest during practice, most likely due to their lack of involvement or simply because of the **tedious nature** of the training session. This often prompted coaches to realign their players' focus, and as one coach clarified during our observations, **"You guys need to listen and pay attention, as we all need to be on the same page if we are going to score goals from this play!".**

But we must understand that a high percentage of coaches unwittingly take this approach simply because again they are repeating what they experienced as youngsters, or when playing at high school or college. Many see these methods taken in professional sports and by other youth coaches so they naturally assume that this is the appropriate action to take. Dr. Paul Ford and colleagues make another insightful point in their study investigating the training activities and instructional behaviors utilized by youth soccer coaches, affirming that, **"When acquiring and designing practice activities and instructional behaviors, coaches tend to rely on emulation of other coaches, their own intuition, and the traditions of the sport, rather than on evidence-based research findings."**[128]

Alarmingly, we observed many paid coaches working for clubs that espouse **player development as their primary objective** focusing on set-plays and team concepts consistently during their training practices with young players. Unfortunately, this is something that many parents who spend significant amounts of money on their child's soccer education often fail to identify, understand, or even question. However, it has been very motivating when we have encountered a few parents identifying this scenario unfold with their child. For example, a parent whose 12 year old son recently came to our program had this to say about their previous experiences with a self-proclaimed leading club:

When we first joined the club, we were told that their main objective was on player development. But I watched my child in that club for two years, and after driving him to practice after practice it became clear that those training sessions did not focus on my child's individual development. They were constantly all about preparing the team for upcoming games and tournaments.

Observation 3: Training Activities were too complex and difficult for young players

A common mistake many coaches make is introducing exercises that are beyond young players' capabilities. During our research we observed numerous drills that kept breaking down because they were simply **too complicated to follow or too technically demanding for young players to execute**. Leading youth soccer coach Horst Wein substantiates this issue when he states, "One problem with most methods of training is that they employ complex situations **before children are ready for them**. Children are asked to face situations that are simply beyond their scope at that particular stage of their development."[129]

Here are two examples that we observed:

*Example 1: A team of 10 and 11 year old players were asked to loft a driven pass to their teammates 30-35 yards apart. After a couple of minutes, **clearly flustered** due to soccer balls not reaching their intended target and flying all over the field hitting players in other groups, the coach stopped play and brought his players in. After speaking with them for a couple of minutes and **venting his frustration**, the coach sent them back out again to perform the same drill.*

*Example 2: With a large amount of cones arranged all over the field, the coach took significant time leading his U10 team through what appeared to be a very complex exercise involving passing and controlling. As he signaled for the drill to begin, the first couple of players immediately passed the ball in the wrong direction, which prompted him to stop and start the exercise again. Once more, the first couple of players could not grasp exactly what he was attempting to implement **which caused the coach to become frustrated and highly animated**. After it quickly broke down on the third attempt, the coach summoned the players in and they began to do **push-ups!***

These two examples suggest that both coaches **misjudged their players' readiness** by a good margin for the demands of the selected activity. For instance, in example 1, it was clear from the onset that some of these youngsters would struggle to execute a 15-20 yard pass with consistent accuracy. Therefore, asking these players to drive a lofted ball twice that distance was always going to be a challenge that they were not technically ready for.

Example 2 was a different situation, as it was not technically overwhelming nor was it a matter of intelligence or game understanding. It was a simply too demanding from a multi-process perspective, as players were overloaded with too many tasks and too much information. After watching the coach go through this drill time and time again we conclude that he must have relayed instructions along the following lines of:

"The first player passes the ball to that cone, and then turns to receive another ball from the red cone and immediately switches with the player on the other side so that he can receive the pass from the left and run onto the next ball. But make sure you receive it side-on and open your hips to the field. Got it?!?!?"

Again, as we witnessed in example 2, what is remarkable is that many coaches become frustrated and annoyed when players fail to execute or comprehend the exercises presented to them even though the drills are too complex. This is another example where coaches deal with mistakes negatively. Additionally, when an exercise is not working many coaches adamantly persist with the same drill and completely reject responsibility for its breaking down.

Once more, utilizing the academic world as an example, how would a parent react who found out that their 10 year old child was **punished** at school for not understanding trigonometry or making calculation errors in algebra because their teacher had presented an academic challenge beyond their current capabilities? What if the teacher then became annoyed with your child because the youth failed to perform this task, continually demanded that they get it right or they would have to do push-ups, and proceeded with the same activity even though they simply could not manage it?

When training is approached in the manner outlined in observations 1, 2, or 3, it will undoubtedly lead to negative consequences for many young players' experiences and development in the sport. This is substantiated through research by leading experts and coaches and will be explained in more detail in the second part of this chapter.

Over the years we have observed many youngsters who have come to our program displaying significant technical limitations and poor decision making skills despite the fact they had been playing for 3 or 4 years; this is especially the case when players have come from environments that focused heavily on **early team success**.

Although many coaches who implement these misguided training practices are simply unaware of how their actions and beliefs negatively impact players' development, these coaching methods simply waste so much valuable training time preventing many young players from laying a solid physical and technical foundation so essential to their progress in the sport. Furthermore, as players are inactive for long spells during practice and their individual progress is neglected, many youngsters naturally become disinterested, frustrated, and disillusioned with their experiences; undoubtedly contributing to the alarming dropout rates witnessed in youth soccer.

Positive training considerations

As the objective of this book is to change the philosophical approach in youth soccer from one where the emphasis is on winning and a premature focus on the team's best interests, to one where the priority is the long-term development of each individual, we will now highlight some positive training aspects that will provide young players the opportunity to cultivate a passion for the game and unlock their true potential.

Young players must enjoy their soccer. **The power of this cannot be underestimated.** Although this is an obvious point to make, and we hear many coaches and parents consistently declare, **"It's got to be fun, that's the main thing"**, we must recognize that this is easier to say than actually put into action, hence why we see so many young players not enjoying their training experiences; especially if they are subjected to any of the approaches we discussed in observations 1, 2, or 3 earlier in the chapter.

Enjoyment has to be the primary objective because if young players are relishing their training they will demonstrate a **desire to come back and continue with their participation**. As organizations, coaches, and parents, we have to remember that for many players their formative years are the critical period when they decide whether they like or dislike playing soccer. So if their initial encounters with the sport are fun, positive, and educational, it is more likely they will fall in love with the game. And once they are captivated by the sport, we can guide and support their development and help them unlock their potential.

Let the players get on with it

As we highlighted earlier in the chapter, one of the key observations we made was how coaches persistently stop practice during training. Again, there will be key moments when coaches need to convey an important coaching message in order to facilitate players understanding and maintain order within a group. The crucial point for all coaches and parents to recognize is that all young players must be provided with significant spells of uninterrupted play in order to help them enjoy and learn.

In light of this, during practice all coaches should aim to **reduce their intervention as much as possible**. In our program we always encourage our coaches to relax, observe, and ensure that the training exercises are running smoothly so that all players enjoy and learn during their practice. Additionally, rather than trying to coach every mistake and guide players through each questionable decision, our coaches simply introduce a theme of what they are looking for at the beginning of each activity and possibly inject a related progressive point later in the session.

We also relay to coaches that they do not have to feel under pressure or obligation to justify their 'coaching expertise', or live up to any stereotype of what a coach should be doing just because people are there watching them. As coaches, we are there to help young players enjoy their experiences and develop effectively, not put on a show to entertain the onlookers!

While visiting Manchester United's training facility we observed how the training environment that was created by their coaches was **primed towards enjoyment and learning**. The striking feature of this visit was that all of the coaches allowed young players the freedom to get on with their training activities, offering only limited instruction and guidance when they felt it was appropriate. If we have leading coaches at the Manchester United academy behaving in such a manner, we must consider they take this approach because they know it is conducive for player development.

We must remember that a key component that contributes to an effective training session for young players is constantly keeping players busy and stimulated. Therefore consistently creating vibrant and lively sessions where young players are buzzing around like bees and constantly engaged in activity *(as opposed to standing around due to lines and lectures)* will have greater impact developmentally.

Keeping group numbers to a minimum during **exercises** (i.e. players working in pairs, three's or four's) helps us in this process. The following example merely demonstrates how coaches can be more effective by simply giving a little thought to the process and implementing exercises using smaller groups.

Exercise 1

Exercise 1 illustrates a common passing drill and method utilized by many coaches in youth soccer. Here we have 12 players working in a group. Each player passes the ball across and follows their pass to join the back of the adjacent line. But due to the large numbers in this group, players touch the ball on a limited basis. Here is the same exercise set up a little more efficiently by using smaller groups.

Exercise 2

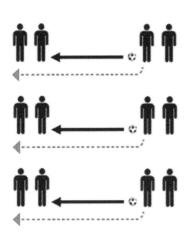

As we can see in this simple example, this approach offers young players more opportunity to touch the ball and be engaged in activity. No matter what exercise you are implementing, always ask whether you can make it more effective by reducing the numbers in each group and offering young players more interaction with the ball.

Note: As a keen eye may have observed, here we could reduce the numbers even further by having three players per group. However, we have to provide players with sufficient recovery time and allow them to get into position.

As we also looked at earlier in the chapter, coaches often setup exercises that are too complicated when working with young players. Consequently, activities can regularly break down, disrupting the flow of their training session. Therefore, when you introduce an exercise it is frequently more effective to keep things as simple as possible at first and increase the level of difficulty based on the players' ability to cope with the challenge. If at any time the activity is not flowing, **have the conviction to quickly change it or move on to the next exercise rather than persevere with an activity that players are clearly struggling with.** This will undoubtedly be a positive step toward ensuring that players are getting on with it.

We have also found that young players display more passion and become far more motivated when they are offered the opportunity to influence what they are doing. For example, we frequently allow young players to referee their own games or collectively decide on their playing positions as this provides them with opportunities for healthy interaction with their peers. Professor Gretchen Kerr of the University of Toronto and her colleague Patricia Miller make reference to this point when investigating the relationship between performance excellence and personal development in sport, stating, "Even very young **athletes should participate in making decisions** in a developmentally appropriate manner. This may be something as simple as choosing between two exercises. As athletes mature, they are provided with greater opportunities to contribute to decision-making."[130]

Develop a physical and technical foundation

Again, one of the biggest mistakes many coaches and parents make is placing the emphasis on the team far too prematurely and neglecting the young players' individual development. When players are young, it is **absolutely essential** for their involvement in the sport and their future progress to provide them with the opportunity to develop a physical and technical foundation.

Many leading development experts and elite coaches recognize how important it is for young players to spend a high percentage of their training time engaged in activity that enhances their **technical development** and **physical literacy** *such as agility, balance, coordination, reflexes, and speed*. This is because fundamental movement skills are the building blocks children need to participate successfully in all types of games, physical activities, and sports. **Furthermore, the development of fundamental movement skills is an important step towards ensuring lifelong involvement in physical activity.**[131]

Arsene Wenger, a successful head coach for Arsenal Football Club of the English Premier League and also renowned for the development of a number of world class soccer players, stresses the importance of a solid technical foundation, "You have to build a player like a house. **If you don't start at the**

basement of the house the rest of the work is useless. The basement of the house is between the ages of 5-12 and this is the most important age to develop players. You have to develop technique by the age of 12."[132]

It is sentiments such as these which confirm why it is so **wasteful and neglectful to spend considerable amounts of training time working on off-side traps and corner kicks with young players just to increase the teams' chances of winning their next game or tournament.**

When players develop a sound foundation in these areas, many become more confident, expressive and naturally more effective at executing the fundamental skills and techniques required in the sport. This is something that we have observed first hand time and time again and is supported by Professor Margaret Whitehead a leading development expert of the University of Liverpool in England who asserts, "Individuals who are physically literate will move with poise, economy and confidence in a wide variety of physically challenging situations."[133]

In reference to developing fundamental movement and technical skills, coaches should be aware of what athletic development experts term '**windows of accelerated adaptation**'. Basically this term refers to a period of time in a young player's development when specific physical and technical capabilities can progress at an accelerated rate with appropriate training activities. Essentially, when coaches provide young players with the opportunity to take advantage of these key moments, they will have a greater chance to maximize their full potential.

It is not our intention to offer a detailed discussion on these windows; and there has been some ambiguity and debate in the academic world regarding the precise time they occur.[134] Again, we must recognize that all players mature and develop at different rates, meaning discrepancies in their progressive needs and training requirements will always exist. By understanding the logic behind this concept we can follow basic guidelines to help us develop young players. According to athletic development experts Dr. Istvan Balyi and Ann Hamilton, the following windows of opportunity exist during the early stages of development:

- The window of accelerated adaptation for **agility, quickness and change of direction** (6-8 years of age for girls; 7-9 years of age for boys).

- The window of accelerated adaptation for **motor coordination** [technical ball skills] (8-11 years of age for girls; 7-12 years of age for boys).[135]

Over the years we have always ensured in our program that players aged 5 – 13 receive significant time to enhance their physical literacy and technical development by using basic exercises in training. There are tremendous amounts of material and resources prescribing how a coach can go about this. The exercises we implement in our program involve aspects such as quick feet, hopping, jumping, balancing, and changing direction with and without a ball. Still, we ensure that players are interacting with the ball for a majority of their training time, as we can incorporate the physical and technical aspects simultaneously. And the most effective way to achieve this is through the use of small sided games.

Utilizing small sided games to enhance player development

During a training practice, the majority of young players love nothing more than simply playing the game. And this is great news! Because not only does it take care of the important necessity of providing players with enjoyment, but it is also is the most effective way for young players to progress from a number of developmental perspectives.

By consistently playing in small sided games (or SSGs as we will refer to them from now on) players are offered an abundance of opportunities to move their bodies at different speeds in various planes of motion, helping them develop their physical literacy. As the number of players on each team is small, the opportunity to touch the ball increases significantly and therefore players receive numerous opportunities to swiftly progress in their technical development.

There are also other important developmental benefits to implementing SSGs, which considerably facilitate the players' improvement. We must be bear in mind that effective performance in soccer is not only dependent on the execution of physical and technical skills, but also on a number of perceptual-cognitive skills that continuously interact in a dynamic way. Here are some important perceptual-cognitive skills young players will develop significantly in SSGs:

- *Recognizing the moment to play, i.e. dribble, change direction, play into a different area, make a pass, take a shot, etc.*

- *Understanding how to deny and exploit space.*

- *Processing early information about the postural position of an opponent/team-mate before making a decision and executing a specific skill.*

- *Problem solving and executing appropriate decisions in a swift fashion.*

- *Being able to do the unexpected and be creative.*

- *Anticipating what actions opponents and teammates will make in a given situation.*

- *Quickly scanning the playing environment for relevant cues, for example pushing forward or dropping defensively.*

So, because effective soccer performance is dependent on the interaction of perceptual, cognitive, technical, and movement skills, it is imperative to offer players ample opportunities to replicate this interaction in their training environment. And as many leading coaches and researchers state, the best way to do this is through the use of SSG activities as they resemble the actual demands of real competitive games.

We have found that the optimum numbers to present players with the most developmental opportunities are 3 v 3, 4 v 4, and 5 v 5. Researcher Richard Fenoglio of Manchester Metropolitan University undertook a pilot study with Manchester United's academy teams and established that these numbers were the most optimal for learning, hence the reason why they spend significant amounts of their training time implementing them with their young players.[136]

Furthermore, researchers Dr. Barry Drust and Steven Jones investigated the benefits of SSGs in youth soccer, concluding that 4 v 4 provides young players with the most developmental opportunities. These researchers confirm, "The number of players should be **carefully considered by coaches** if the development of players is important. Activities that include small numbers of players deliver a more effective **multi-component training stimulus.**"[137]

Implementing small sided games is the most powerful way to elevate enjoyment levels and enhance players' all-round progress.

But how much time should coaches dedicate to SSG activity with young players?

Throughout our coaching experiences we have consistently dedicated a high percentage of training time to SSGs as we have always felt they were very productive. We established that there are a number of developmental experts who advocate that **the majority of training time** should be devoted to SSG activity not only because physical, technical, and cognitive skills are enriched, but because they also feel that if mistakes are made during SSGs, players will learn more effectively due to these mistakes being made in actual games. *This provides further evidence supporting how mistakes are important for young players' development and learning, and that mistakes should be embraced positively.*

Because we encounter many young players with a wide range of physical and technical capability in our program, we have always questioned how much SSG activity we should offer novice players *(including players new to the sport who find it extremely difficult to control the ball under no pressure)* in comparison to players who have developed a more advanced movement and technical foundation. In order to further our insight on this topic and confirm that our intuition regarding SSGs was headed in the right direction, we contacted researcher Richard Fenoglio due to his work with Manchester United on this matter, explaining to him our program, the various levels of capability of the players we worked with, and our objectives. Richard made some points that really facilitated our understanding. First, he confirmed that all young players will benefit from high percentages of SSG involvement, which could consist of up to **approximately 80% of their training time**. He also acknowledged our need to offer novice players increased opportunities to develop their physical and technical attributes in a less demanding setting (i.e. outside of the SSG context with no pressure from opposing players).

We have always found it useful to offer young players with limited movement and technical skills increased opportunities to improve these facets of the game using **basic exercises outside of the SSG context**. These activities include players consistently having a ball at their feet while executing changes of direction and movement skills, as they attempt to remain in control of the ball. The key point that we focus on when setting up these exercises is that players have lots of touches on the ball, often working individually or with groups of 2 and 3 to maximize their involvement and limit the levels of inactivity. **We then increase their levels of SSG activity as soon as they become**

competent in their basic movement and technical skills. Therefore, it is essential that we monitor **each individual's progress.**

Another important consideration is being **creative with the SSG format**. Changing the dynamic of these games allows us to appropriately adjust the level of challenge to make it more enjoyable, stimulating, and beneficial from a learning perspective for all players. There are various ways this can be done. For example, offering players larger areas to play in allows them more time to control the ball and make decisions. And utilizing overload situations, such as 5 v 3, offers the players (on the team of 5) more opportunity to implement skills while increasing game understanding in comparison to what they would face in a 5 v 5 scenario.

Conversely, we can make the playing area smaller to create a tighter situation. This requires the players' first touch to be precise and their decisions to be made quicker which enhances their problem solving capabilities. We can also add more goals for them to score in to encourage players to drive into different areas of the field and change direction or the point of attack.

SSG activity is a fundamental component which must be heavily utilized in training. However, many coaches consistently deny their young players sufficient opportunities to participate in SSG activity because again they spend the majority of practice robotically implementing drill after drill or working prematurely on team concepts. And even if they do allocate a certain amount of time for a game *(which is frequently in a format that does not even qualify as a SSG and involves number such as 8 v 8 or higher)* it is only for the last 10 minutes of practice or traditionally as a reward for players' **good behavior or cooperation** during training.

A commitment to consistent practice

The discussions in this chapter have primarily centered on how coaches should approach training to ensure that players enjoy their experiences, so that we can retain them in the sport and provide them with effective developmental opportunities. But as we are discussing training considerations we feel it is beneficial and applicable to highlight the amount of practice required to become an elite performer in the sport.

According to researchers Dr. K. Anders Ericsson and Professor Neil Charness, approximately **10,000 hours of practice** *(referred to as the "10,000 rule")* are required to reach elite levels of performance in many domains including soccer.[138] This premise is supported by significant research. For example, Dr. Werner Helsen and colleagues investigated the number of hours that professional, semi-professional, and amateur soccer players in Europe had accumulated over a span of 18 years. The players studied were approximately 24 years of age, meaning many of them began playing around the age of 6. They established that the professional players had accumulated **9,332 hours**, the semi-professional **7,449 hours**, and the amateur players accumulated **5,079 hours**.[139]

What was also discovered was the amount of time spent in team practice was the strongest discriminator across skill groups. The professional players spent more time in **individual practice** than the semi-professional and amateur players during the ages 6 to 12. Again, this provides evidence why young players should not be spending their important years doing what is best for the team if the objective is on player development.

Additionally, between the ages of 10-18 young players at the Ajax academy in Holland and in Barcelona's La Masia facility, which adopted the highly successful Ajax development model under former Barcelona coach Johan Cruyff in the early-1990s, can expect to receive 7,000-8,000 hours of coaching.[140] Therefore, is it no surprise that Barcelona has produced players of outstanding ability such as Xavi, Andres Iniesta and Lionel Messi in recent years. We must also recognize that due to their love for the game these players likely **spent many additional hours honing their skills in their own time.** We often hear the testimonies of mothers and fathers who recollect accounts of how today's superstars of the game constantly had a **ball at their feet** and played in the back yard, street, or local park **without intervention** from an early age. And as the 10,000 hours of practice can be comprised of structured or unstructured activity at home, at school, or in other settings, Xavi's, Iniesta's, and Messi's accumulated time of soccer participation was likely well beyond 10,000 hours by the time they reached adulthood.

In order to place this into context, reaching 10,000 hours of practice would mean approximately:

- *3 hours of practice per day for just over 9 years.*

- *2 hours of practice per day for almost 14 years.*

- *1.5 hours of practice per day for just over 18 years.*

When we look at the research and evidence related to the 10,000 rule, it is easy to understand why young players subjected to:

1. *travelling ridiculous distances and having to spend 4-8 hours in a car to play in tournaments*
2. *wasting valuable training time stood in line or because the coach continually intervenes*
3. *sitting on the bench during games because the coach is placing the emphasis on winning and they are not considered to be someone who can help reach that objective 'today'*
4. *working on corner kicks in training and other team concepts for prolonged spells*
5. *missing training on a consistent basis*

will simply waste crucial hours and opportunities to accumulate the necessary practice time that will allow them to reach higher levels of competence.

Over the years, a key issue that we have observed in our program is that many players who take time off from our training for 2-6 months or more often return at a less developed state than when they left *(this is often magnified as many players who are taking long spells away from soccer have not been engaging in much soccer activity in their own time)*. Although we always strive to de-emphasize player comparisons, many young players naturally compare themselves to their peers, often concluding that those peers who continued to practice consistently while they spent considerable time away progressed further in their development, **especially in technical areas**. This frequently leaves many returning players feeling de-motivated and questioning their own ability and involvement in the sport.

Some parents believe that if their children stop participating in soccer for a few months, they will *automatically* be able to pick up where they left off when they return. **In the majority of cases this is a completely misguided perception**. When players have trained consistently in our program over a 3 month period in comparison to a player who has not trained at all during this time frame, they will have trained approximately **40-50 more times** in an environment where technical development is a major priority. So, one can expect that these players who kept training will have made considerable strides in comparison to those who have not trained at all.

Many development experts and elite coaches appreciate the **power of consistent training**. In their study investigating practice, instruction and skill acquisition in soccer, researchers Professor Mark Williams and Dr. Nicola Hodges assert:

> The crucial point is that while hereditary factors are likely to play a role in shaping an individual's response to practice and training, skills are highly modifiable and adaptable to training and every player will need to practice for many hours to develop and **refine these skills. What is underestimated is the specific amount of practice needed.**[141]

Furthermore, as athletic development expert Dr. Istvan Balyi points out, "A long-term commitment to training is required to produce athletes in all sports, something that needs to be communicated to and understood by coaches, parents and sports administrators."[142]

Therefore, when a young player has taken significant time off from training we strongly recommend they receive the following words of guidance:

"When you go back to soccer training, remember that those players you played with before have continued to train. So don't expect to be at the same level as them. That's not important anyway! Just go back enjoy yourself and begin learning again."

Chapter Nine

Final Thoughts and Red Flags

"Smart coaches are continually updating their knowledge, so they can adjust their work accordingly. Less enlightened coaches keep on doing what they've done for 30 years, because they think they already know all there is to know about coaching. They are not good learners themselves. They never stop and take a long hard look at their own effectiveness."[143]

When coaching young players, it is our duty to develop their passion for soccer by providing them with enjoyment, positive experiences, and learning opportunities no matter what their current capabilities are. Taking this approach will undoubtedly allow us to reach the main objective of encouraging more players to remain in the game. But we must also recognize that by taking the positive steps that we have outlined in each chapter we will help players develop a solid foundation and increase their chances of becoming more effective soccer players in the long-term. Therefore, we should always work off the premise: **Develop the passion so that we can develop the player.**

In light of the issues we have discussed, it is also clear why so many young players are having bad experiences and dropping out of the sport at an early age. As we have outlined, it is evident why so many young players fail to receive the opportunity to unlock their true potential in the sport. Therefore, as coaches and parents, we must make a positive difference by encouraging those involved in youth soccer to eradicate this conventional approach and begin to implement the thoughts of developmental experts, elite coaches, and leading figures.

We felt it would be helpful to end with a section which allows parents to **instantly identify** whether or not a club or coach is truly placing the main emphasis on player development with their child, or whether the club or coach is taking the conventional approach and focusing primarily on winning and immediate team success at the expense of young players' experiences and progress. This will also help establish whether you or other parents are facilitating a positive learning environment, or whether the development process is being disrupted due to misguided actions or beliefs.

Finally, from a coach's perspective, if you find yourself, a colleague, or parent performing any of the following actions, it is certainly time to reflect and make a change.

Based on all the issues we have discussed in this book, here are a number of **'red flags'** that arise when the conventional approach is taken. If you witness any of these inappropriate actions during the early stages of development, **you must be proactive and challenge the person or organization responsible. This is the only way we are going to make a positive difference.**

Red Flags

- *A coach or parent demonstrates noticeable anger or frustration when the team gives up a goal or displays too much jubilation when their team scores.*

- *The coach consistently approaches games with winning as the main objective.*

- *The coach consistently hypes up the importance of game results with big pre-game speeches.*

- *A coach or parent spends significant amounts of time analyzing the team or players' performance after a game.*

- *A coach or parent displays anger or frustration because the team lost.*

- *The club constantly promotes winning results and trophy success on their website.*

- *A coach or parent constantly shouts, directs, and instructs players from the sidelines.*

- *A coach or parent deals with mistakes negatively through scolding, making critical comments or being sarcastic, and/or expressing anger.*

- *The coach 'pigeonholes' players into set positions week after week.*

- *The more advanced players are always positioned in central areas of the field where they can have the greatest impact on the game.*

- *The coach constantly attempts to hide less advanced players in positions where there is less chance they will be engaged in the play - e.g. wide areas of the field.*

- *The coach consistently offers the more advanced players greater percentages of playing time.*

- *The coach leaves the less advanced players on the sidelines for long spells.*

- *The coach promotes a 'fight for your place' mentality between players.*

- *The coach has a '3 goal player' who only plays if the team is up by 3 goals or is losing by 3 goals due to the game's impending conclusion.*

- *A club, coach, or parent espouses the idea that every player needs to play against the 'best players' or 'best competition' in order to develop effectively.*

- *The coach has the entire team playing up in age group even though some players are unready for that level of challenge.*

- *A player who demonstrates advanced capabilities is denied a more stimulating challenge which meets his or her progressive needs.*

- *The coach never offers players the opportunity to have input or share their perspectives.*

- *A club, coach, or parent goes to great lengths to recruit players.*

- *You are handed a "You have been identified" card by a coach or club representative.*

- *A club utilizes tryout procedures in an attempt to identify players who can bring them immediate success.*

- *The coach repeatedly intervenes during training sessions and talks for long spells of time.*

- *The coach subjects players to prolonged inactive spells during training, often due to their standing in line.*

- *To improve the team's chances of winning their next game, the coach focuses on team tactics and concepts during training, e.g. corner kicks, set-plays, off-side traps.*

- *During training, the coach consistently attempts to implement complicated drills that the players are clearly unready for.*

- *The coach discards or neglects a player because the player does not display favorable physical characteristics.*

- *A coach or parent makes a subjective assumption about a young player's future success in the game.*

- *A club, coach, or parent promotes tournaments as a critical requirement to take players to the 'next level.'*

- *A club administrator or coach tells you not to read this book!*

References

1. Galbraith, J. K. (1988) Baseball: Socialist as Apple Pie, The New York Times, accessed online at: http://www.nytimes.com/1988/08/07/opinion/baseball-socialist-as-apple-pie.html

2. Twain, M. (2002) In: Icke, D. *Alice in Wonderland and the World Trade Center Disaster Why the Official Story of 9/11 is a Monumental Lie*, p.316, Wildwood, Bridge of Love Publications.

3. Williams, A. M., Hodges, N. J. (2005) Practice, Instruction and Skill Acquisition in Soccer: Challenging Tradition, *Journal of Sports Sciences*, 23(6), pp. 637-650.

4. Snow, S. In: Scavuzzo, D. (2012) Experts on Soccer Player Development Give Blue Print for Youth Clubs and Coaches, SoccerNation.com, accessed online at: http://www.soccernation.com/experts-on-soccer-player-development-give-blue-print-for-youth-clubs-and-coaches-cms-2331

5. Martin, J. (2012) Youth Soccer: The Good, the Bad and the Ugly, NSCAA Soccer Journal, 57(3), p.5, Kansas City, National Soccer Coaches Association of America.

6. Ibid.

7. Weinberg, R. S., Gould, D. (2007) *Foundations of Sports and Exercise Psychology 4th Ed.* Champaign, Illinois, Human Kinetics.

8. Engh, F. (2002) *Why Johnny Hates Sports*, pp. 3-4, New York, Square One Publishers.

9. Smoll, F. L., Cumming, S. P., Smith, R. E. (2011) Enhancing Coach-Parent Relationships in Youth Sports: Increasing Harmony and Minimizing Hassle*, International Journal of Sports Science and Coaching*, 6(1), pp. 13-25.

10. Martens, R. (2004) *Successful Coaching 3rd Ed.* p.20, Champaign, Illinois, Human Kinetics.

11. Howe, B. Tournament Play - Good or Bad?, World of Soccer.com, accessed online at:
    http://www.worldofsoccer.com/index.php?option=com_content&task=view&id=720&Itemid=2

12. Stratton, G., Reilly, T., Williams, A. M., Richardson, D. (2004) *Youth Soccer: From Science to Performance*, pp. 2-3, Oxon, Routledge.

13. Hinton, K. Competition and Cooperation: Helping Youth Strike a Balance, Cooperative Extension Fact Sheet, University of Nevada, accessed online at:
    http://www.unce.unr.edu/publications/files/cy/other/fs9386.pdf

14. Thorpe, R. In: Kidman, L. (2005) Rod Thorpe on Teaching Games for Understanding, Athlete-centered Coaching: Developing Inspired and Inspiring People, Christchurch, Innovative Print Communications Ltd.

15. Vargas-Tonsing, T. M. (2009) An exploratory examination of the effects of coaches' pre-game speeches on athletes' perceptions of self-efficacy and emotion, *Journal of Sport Behavior*, 32(1), pp. 92-111.

16. Sage, L., Kavusannu, M. (2008) Goal Orientations, Motivational Climate and Moral Behavior in Youth Soccer: Exploring their Temporal Stability and Reciprocal Relationships, *Journal of Sports Sciences*, 26(7), pp. 717-732.

17. Weinberg, R. S., Gould, D. (2007) *Foundations of Sports and Exercise Psychology 4th Ed.* p.517, Champaign, Illinois, Human Kinetics.

18. Giles, K. B. In: Gambetta, V. (2006) Interview with Kelvin Giles, Functional Path Training Blog, accessed online at:
    http://functionalpathtraining.blogspot.com/2006/08/kelvin-giles-interview.html

19. Wein, H. (2007) *Developing Youth Football Players, Tap the Full Potential of Your Young Footballers*, p. 3, Champaign, Illinois, Human Kinetics.

20. Cumming, S. P., Ewing, M. E. (1999) Parental Involvement in Youth Sports: The Good, the Bad and the Ugly!, *Spotlight on Youth Sports*, 26(1), pp. 1-5.

21. Seefeldt, V., Ewing, M., Walk, S. (1992) Overview of Youth Sports Programs in the United States, Washington, *Carnegie Council on Adolescent Development.*

22. Bloom, B. S. (1985) *Developing Talent in Young People*, London, Random House Publishing.

23. Schellscheidt, M. In: Woitalla, M. (2012) Thanks, Manny Schellscheidt!, Socceramerica.com, accessed online at: http://www.socceramerica.com/article/45147/thanks-manny-schellscheidt.html

24. Smoll, F. L., Cumming, S. P., Smith, R. E. (2011) Enhancing Coach-Parent Relationships in Youth Sports: Increasing Harmony and Minimizing Hassle, *International Journal of Sports Science and Coaching*, 6(1), pp. 13-25.

25. Baker, J., Horton, S., Robertson-Wilson, J., Wall, M. (2003) Nurturing Expertise: Factors Influencing the Development of Elite Athlete, *Journal of Sports Science & Medicine*, 2, pp. 1-9.

26. Smith, M., Cushion, C. J. (2006) An Investigation of the In-Game Behaviors of Professional, Top-Level Youth Soccer Coaches, *Journal of Sports Sciences*, 24(4), pp. 355-366.

27. Holt, N. (2002) A Comparison of the Soccer Talent Development Systems in England and Canada, *European Physical Education Review*, 8(3), pp. 270-285.

28. Santisteban, J. In: Roxburgh, A. (2006) The Da Vinci Coach, p.3, *The Technician*, Nyon, UEFA.

29. Ibid

30. Whitmore, J. (2009) *Coaching for Performance: Growing Human Potential and Purpose, 4th Ed.*, p.10, London, Nicholas Brealey Publishing.

31. Williams, A. M., Hodges, N. J. (2005) Practice, Instruction and Skill Acquisition in Soccer: Challenging Tradition, *Journal of Sports Sciences*, 23(6), pp. 637-650.

32. Smoll, F. L., Cumming, S. P., Smith, R. E. (2011) Enhancing Coach-Parent Relationships in Youth Sports: Increasing Harmony and Minimizing Hassle, *International Journal of Sports Science and Coaching*, 6(1), pp. 13-25.

33. Wein, H. (2007) *Developing Youth Football Players, Tap the Full Potential of Your Young Footballers*, p.5, Champaign, Illinois, Human Kinetics.

34. Martindale, R. J. J., Collins, D., Abraham, A. (2007) Effective Talent Development: The Elite Coach Perspective in UK Sport, *Journal of Applied Sport Psychology*, 19(2), pp. 187-206.

35. Peacock, J. (2004) Dribbling, *Insight*, The FA Coaches Association Journal, Autumn-Winter 2004, pp. 34-38, London, FA Learning.

36. Reyna, C., Woitalla, M. (2004) *More than Goals: The Journey from Backyard Games to World Cup Competition*, p.14, Champaign, Illinois, Human Kinetics.

37. Fraser-Thomas, J., Côtè, J., Deakin, J. (2008) Examining Adolescent Sport Dropout and Prolonged Engagement from a Developmental Perspective, *Journal of Applied Sport Psychology*, 20(3), pp. 318-333.

38. Omli, J., La Voi, N. M. (2009) Background Anger in Youth Sport: A Perfect Storm?, *Journal of Sport Behavior*, 32(2), pp. 242-260.

39. Kannekens, R., Elferink-Gemser, M. T., Visscher C. (2011) Positioning and Deciding: Key Factors for Talent Development in Soccer, *Scandinavian Journal of Medicine & Science in Sports,* 21(6), pp. 846–852.

40. Landsorp, R. In Coyle, D. (2009) *The Talent Code: Greatness Isn't Born. It's Grown. Here's How*, p.195, New York, Bantam Books.

41. Smith, M., Cushion, C.J. (2006) An Investigation of the in-game Behaviors of Professional, Top-Level Youth Soccer Coaches, *Journal of Sports Sciences*, 24(4), pp. 355-366.

42. Brooking, T. In: White, J. (2008) Trevor Brooking: Concentrate on Grassroots, The Telegraph, accessed online at:
http://www.telegraph.co.uk/sport/football/world-cup-

2010/teams/england/2290669/Trevor-Brooking-Concentrate-on-grassroots.html

43. Messi, L. In: Gardner, P (2011) Messi explains his artistry: I play like a child, Socceramerica.com, accessed online at: http://www.socceramerica.com/article/41936/messi-explains-his-artistry-i-play-like-a-child.html

44. Cruyff, J. In: Ruiz.L. (2001) Soccer *Secrets to Success Things Great Players and Coaches Should Know*, p.8, Spring City, Pennsylvania, Reedswain Publishing.

45. Salmela, J. H., Moraes, L. C. (2004) Coaching, Families and Learning in Brazilian Youth Football Players, *Insight*, The FA Coaches Association Journal, Spring 2004, pp. 36-37, London, FA Learning.

46. Jennings, J., Malcak, L. N. (2004) *Communication Basics*, p.125, Alexandria, American Society for Training and Development.

47. Trapatonni, G. In: Collina, P. (2004) *The Rules of the Game*, p. 193, Pan MacMillan, London.

48. Gervis, M., Dunn, N. (2004) The Emotional Abuse of Elite Child Athletes By Their Coaches, *Child Abuse Review*, Vol. 13(3), pp. 215-223.

49. Ibid

50. Bickerton, P. (2005) You can do it if you really want , TES, accessed online at: http://www.tes.co.uk/teaching-resource/You-can-do-it-if-you-really-want-2145566

51. Claxton, G. In: Allpress, J. (2006) Smart Coaching Managing Mistakes to the Players Advantage, *Insight*, The FA Coaches Association Journal, Spring-Summer 2006, pp. 31-35, London, FA Learning.

52. Smith, M., Cushion, C. J. (2006) An Investigation of the in-game Behaviors of Professional, Top-Level Youth Soccer Coaches, *Journal of Sports Sciences*, 24(4), pp. 355-366.

53. Allpress, J. (2006) Smart Coaching Managing Mistakes to the Players Advantage, *Insight*, The FA Coaches Association Journal, Spring-Summer 2006, pp. 31-35, London, FA Learning.

54. Kennedy, J.F. Quoted In: Encyclopædia Britannica, accessed online at: http://www.britannica.com/EBchecked/topic/314791/John-F-Kennedy/314791suppinfo/Supplemental-Information

55. Mulliner, I. 'Player Development versus Team Performance', accessed online at: http://ebookbrowse.com/player-development-versus-team-performance-pdf-d264733873

56. Reyna, C., Woitalla, M. (2004) *More than Goals: The Journey from Backyard Games to World Cup Competition*, pp. 20-21, Champaign, Illinois, Human Kinetics.

57. Mourinho, J. (2008) Football for Kids DVD, Exercise 2: Ball Possession - Communication and Concentration, Yeti Broadcasting, accessed online at: http://www.youtube.com/watch?v=YN33Jvk0rqs

58. Siedentop, D. Hastie, P. A. van der Mars, H. (2004) Complete Guide to Sport Education, Volume 1, p.73, Champaign, Illinois, Human Kinetics.

59. Frankl, D. (2002) Recruiting Practices in Youth Sports: Who's Winning?, California State University, accessed online at: http://instructional1.calstatela.edu/dfrankl/CURR/kin380/PDF/Recruiting-in-Youth_Soccer.pdf

60. Helsen, W. F. Starkes, J.L. Van Winckel, J. (1998) The Influence of Relative Age Effect on Success and Dropout in Male Soccer Players, *American Journal of Human Biology*, 10(6), pp. 791-798.

61. Hodson, A. (1999) Too Much Too Soon? The Risk of 'Overuse' Injuries in Young Football Players, *Journal of Bodywork and Movement Therapies*, 3(2), pp. 85-91.

62. Stewart, C. Meyers, M.C. (2004) Motivational Traits of Elite Youth Soccer Players, *The Physical Educator*, 61(4), pp. 213-218.

63. Ommundsen, Y. Roberts, G.C. Lemyre, P.N. Miller, B.W. (2005) Peer Relationships in Adolescent Competitive Soccer: Associations to Perceived Motivational Climate, Achievement Goals and Perfectionism, *Journal of Sports Sciences*, 23(9), pp. 977-989.

64. Martindale, R.J.J. Collins, D. Abraham, A. (2007) Effective Talent Development: The Elite Coach Perspective in UK Sport, *Journal of Applied Sports Psychology*, 19(2), pp. 187-206.

65. Kershaw, L. In: Winter, H. (2005) 'Youngster's Learning Curve', The Telegraph, accessed online at: http://www.telegraph.co.uk/sport/columnists/henrywinter/2366045/Youngsters-learning-curve.html

66. Simmons, C. (2004) Fast Tracking and Player Development, *Insight*, The FA Coaches Association Journal, Summer 2004, pp. 24-25, London, FA Learning.

67. Meylan, C. Cronin, J. Oliver, J. Hughes, M. (2010) Talent Identification in Soccer: The Role of Maturity Status on Physical, Psychological and Technical Characteristics, *International Journal of Sports Science and Coaching*, 5(4), pp. 571-592.

68. Barnsley, R. H. Thompson, A. H. Legault, P. (1992) Family Planning: Football Style. The Relative Age Effect in Football, *International Review for the Sociology of Sport*, 27(1), pp. 77-87.

69. Helsen, W.F. Starkes, J.L. Van Winckel, J. (2000) Effect of a Change in Selection Year on Success in Male Soccer Players, *American Journal of Human Biology*, 12(6), pp. 729-735.

70. Vincent, J. Glamser, F. D. (2006) Gender Differences in the Relative Age Effect Among US Olympic Development Program Youth Soccer Players, *Journal of Sports Sciences*, 24(4), pp. 405-413.

71. Glamser, F.D. Vincent, J. (2004) The Relative Effect Among Elite American Youth Soccer Players, *Journal of Sport Behavior*, 27(1), pp. 31-38.

72. Philippaerts, R.M. Vaeyens, R. Janssens, M. Van Renterghem, B. Matthys, D. Craen, R. et. al. (2006) The Relationship between Peak Height Velocity and Physical Performance in Youth Soccer Players, *Journal of Sport Sciences*, 24(3), pp. 221-230.

73. Helsen, W. Van Winckel, J. Williams, A.M. (2005) The Relative Age Effect in Youth Soccer Across Europe, *Journal of Sports Sciences*, 23(6), pp. 629-636.

74. Jimenez, I.P. Pain, M. T.G. (2008) Relative Age Effect in Spanish Association Football: It`s Extent and Implications for Wasted Potential, *Journal of Sports Sciences*, 26(10), pp. 995-1003.

75. US Youth Soccer (2012) US Youth Soccer Player Development Model, Chicago, Illinois, US Youth Soccer Coaching Education Department, accessed online at: http://www.usyouthsoccer.org/news/us_youth_soccer_debuts_player_development_model/?story_id=6415

76. Giles, K. B. (2006) Developing Physical Competence: The Cornerstone of LTAD - Part One, p.12, Movement Dynamics, accessed online at: http://movementdynamics.com/uploads/pdfs/physical-competence.pdf

77. Vestberg, T. Gustafson, R. Maurex, L. Ingvar, M. Petrovic, P. (2012) Executive Functions Predict the Success of Top-Soccer Players, *PLoS One*, 7(4), pp. 1-5.

78. McCay, J. T. In: How to Reach Your Potential – Sitting, Volleyball Canada, accessed online at: http://www.vcdm.org/athletes/view/active-start-fundamentals1

79. Horn, T. S. (2011) Enhancing Coach-Parent Relationships in Youth Sports: Increasing Harmony and Minimizing Hassle, A Commentary, *International Journal of Sports Science and Coaching*, 6(1), pp. 27-31.

80. Davids, K. Lees, A. Burwitz, L. (2000) Understanding and Measuring Coordination and Control in Kicking Skills in Soccer: Implications for Talent Identification and Skill Acquisition, *Journal of Sports Sciences*, 18(9), pp. 703-714.

81. Martindale, R.J.J. Collins, D. Abraham, A. (2007) Effective Talent Development: The Elite Coach Perspective in UK Sport, *Journal of Applied Sports Psychology*, 19(2), pp. 187-206.

82. Nash, C. S. Sproule, J. Horton, P. (2008) Sports Coaches` Perceived Role Frames and Philosophies, *International Journal of Sports Science and Coaching*, 3(4), pp. 539-554.

83. De Jong, R, In: Sokolove, M. (2010) How a Soccer Star is Made, The New York Times Magazine, accessed online at: http://www.nytimes.com/2010/06/06/magazine/06Soccer-t.html?pagewanted=all

84. Whitmore, J. (2009) *Coaching for Performance Growing Human Potential and Purpose 4th Ed.*, p.11, London, Nicholas Brealey Publishing.

85. Wein, H. (2007) *Developing Youth Football Players, Tap the Full Potential of Your Young Footballers*, p.viii, Champaign, Illinois, Human Kinetics.

86. Harris, S. Readiness to Participate in Sports, In: Sullivan J.A, Anderson S.J. (2000) *Care of the Young Athlete*, p. 19, Rosemont, Illinois: American Academy of Orthopaedic Surgeons and American Academy of Pediatrics.

87. Daniels, A. M. (2007) Cooperation versus Competition: Is There Really Such an Issue?, *New Directions for Youth Development*, 115, Fall 2007, pp. 43-56.

88. Giles, K. (2006) Interview with Kelvin Giles, Functional Path Training Blog, accessed online at: http://functionalpathtraining.blogspot.com/2006/08/kelvin-giles-interview.html

89. Wein, H. (2007) *Developing Youth Football Players, Tap the Full Potential of Your Young Footballers*, p.2, Champaign, Illinois, Human Kinetics.

90. Ommundsen, Y. Roberts, G. C. Lemyre, P. N. Miller, B.W. (2005) Peer Relationships in Adolescent Competitive Soccer: Associations to Perceived Motivational Climate, Achievement Goals and Perfectionism, *Journal of Sports Sciences*, 23(9), pp. 977-989

91. Csikszentmihalyi, M. Rathunde, K. Whalen, S. (1997) *Talented Teenagers The Roots of Success and Failure*, Cambridge, Cambridge University Press.

92. Brenner, J. S. (2007) Overuse Injuries, Overtraining, and Burnout in Child and Adolescent Athletes, *Pediatrics*, 119(6), pp. 1242-1245.

93. Wiersma, L. (2005) In: Positive Parenting for Youth Soccer, US Youth Soccer, p.21, accessed online at: http://www.dynamosc.com/docs/parent_ed_presentationFINAL_II.pdf

94. Mandingo, J.L. Holt, N.L. (1999) Intrinsically Motivating Children Putting Theory Into Practice: How Cognitive Evaluation Theory Can Help Us Better Understand How To Motivate Children In Physical Activity Environments, Brock University, accessed online at: http://spartan.ac.brocku.ca/~jmandigo/cet.pdf

95. Snow, S. (2008) Active Coaching and Playing Up, US Youth Soccer Blog, accessed online at: http://ysr341.americaneagle.com/soccermonth/blog.asp?blogger_id=5&topic_id=&post_year=2008&post_month=10&print=y

96. Ibid

97. Dilts, R., Bacon Dilts, D. Coaching at the Identity Level, NLP Institute of California, accessed online at: http://www.nlpca.com/DCweb/Coaching_At_The_Identity_Level.html

98. Percy, W. In: Khon, A. (1992) *No Contest The Case Against Competition Why We Lose in Our Race to Win*, p. 1, New York, Houghton Mifflin Company.

99. US Youth Soccer (2012) US Youth Soccer Player Development Model, Chicago, Illinois, US Youth Soccer Coaching Education Department, accessed online at: http://www.usyouthsoccer.org/news/us_youth_soccer_debuts_player_development_model/?story_id=6415

100. Martin, J. Stop the Tournaments, New York State West Youth Soccer Association, accessed online at: http://www.nyswysa.org/coaching/articles/04.html

101. Schmid, S. In: Woog, D. (2002) The Pros and Cons of Tournament Play, *Soccer America*, Vol. 57(11), No. 1530, pp. 48-49, Berkeley, CA, Soccer America.

102. Howe, B. Tournament Play - Good or Bad?, World of Soccer.com, accessed online at: http://www.worldofsoccer.com/index.php?option=com_content&task=view&id=720&Itemid=2

103. Snow, S. (2008) Beware of Tournamentitis, Soccer America, accessed online at: http://www.socceramerica.com/article/25076/beware-of-tournamentitis.html

104. Reyna, C. In: Woitalla, M. (2011) Claudio Reyna: Coaches should sit down, Soccer America, accessed online at: http://www.socceramerica.com/article/41990/claudio-reyna-coaches-should-sit-down.html

105. Balyi, I., Way, R. (2008) Competition is a Good Servant but a Poor Master, Canadian Sport for Life, accessed online at: http://canadiansportforlife.ca/sites/default/files/resources/Competition%20is%20a%20Good%20Servant%2C%20but%20a%20Poor%20Master.pdf

106. Snow, S. (2008) Beware of Tournamentitis, Soccer America, accessed online at: http://www.socceramerica.com/article/25076/beware-of-tournamentitis.html

107. Harwood, C., Knight, C. (2008) Understanding Parental Stressors: An Investigation of British Tennis-Parents, *Journal of Sport Sciences*, 27(4), pp. 339-351.

108. Abrams, D. E., (2002) The Challenge Facing Parents and Coaches in Youth Sports: Assuring Children Fun and Equal Opportunity, *Villanova Sports and Entertainment Law Journal*, Villanova University, 1-33, accessed online at: http://www.thecenterforkidsfirst.org/pdf/DougAbrams.pdf

109. Hawkins, D., Metheny, J. (2001) Overuse Injuries in Youth Sports: Biomechanical Considerations, *Medicine and Science in Sports and Exercise*, 33(10), pp. 1701-1707.

110. Brenner, J. S. (2007) Overuse Injuries, Overtraining, and Burnout in Child and Adolescent Athletes, *Pediatrics*, 119(6), 1242-1245.

111. Howe, B. Howe, B. Tournament Play - Good or Bad?, World of Soccer.com, accessed online at: http://www.worldofsoccer.com/index.php?option=com_content&task=view&id=720&Itemid=2

112. Dupont, G., Nedelec, .M., McCall, A., McCormack, D., Berthoin, S., Wisløff, U. (2010) Effect of 2 Soccer Matches in a Week on Physical Performance and Injury Rate, *The American Journal of Sport Medicine*, 38(9), pp. 1752-1758.

113. Abrahamson, B. (2008) Overuse Injuries in Soccer and Factors That Increase Risk of Injury, *Performance Physical Therapy*, Vol. 2(7), pp. 1-4, accessed online at: http://www.performance-physicaltherapy.com/PDF/PPTnewsletter2008-7.pdf

114. Meyer, N. Soccer Nutrition, Spain Park Soccer, accessed online at: http://www.spainparksoccer.com/assets/soccer%20nutrition.pdf

115. Macedonio, M. Soccer: Energy for Tournaments, Gatorade Sports Science Institute, accessed online at: http://www.gssiweb.com/Article_Detail.aspx?articleid=750

116. Ganio, M. S., Casa, D. J., Yeargin, S. W., McDermott, B. P., Levreault, M. L., Decher, N. R., et.al. (2006) Sweat Rate, Fluid Consumption, and Hydration Indices for Youth Soccer Players: Effects of Educational Intervention, *Medicine and Science in Sports and Exercise*, 38(5S), pp. 110-111.

117. American Dietetic Association (2006) Fueling Soccer Players, University of the Cumberlands, accessed online at: http://www.cumberlandspatriots.com/stats/Athletic%20Training/Soccer.pdf

118. American Academy of Pediatrics, Climatic Heat Stress and the Exercising Child and Adolescent, *Pediatrics*, 106(1), pp. 158-159.

119. Dewaizen, K., In: Woog, D. (2001) CYSA-North bans tournaments, Soccer America, Vol. 56(9), No. 1495, pp. 20-21, Berkeley, CA, Soccer America.

120. Von Herder, J. G. In: Grothe, M. (2008) *I Never Metaphor I Didn't Like a Comprehensive Compilation of History's Greatest Analogies, Metaphors, and Smiles*, p.36, New York, Harper Collins.

121. Reyna, C. Woitalla, M. (2004) *More than Goals: The Journey from Backyard Games to World Cup Competition*, p. 15, Champaign, Illinois, Human Kinetics.

122. Ford, P. R., Yates, I., Williams, A. M. (2010) An Analysis of Practice Activities and Instructional Behaviours used by Youth Soccer Coaches during Practice: Exploring the Link between Science and Application, *Journal of Sports Sciences*, 28(5), pp. 483-495.

123. Keane, R. (2002) *Keane The Autobiography*, p.119, London, Penguin Books.

124. Martindale, J.J. Collins, D. Abraham, A. (2007) Effective Talent Development: The Elite Coach Perspective in UK Sport, Journal of Applied Sports Psychology, 19:2, pp. 187-206.

125. Mulliner, I. Player Development versus Team Performance, Lancaster DewPew Soccer Club, accessed online at: http://www.lancasterdepewsoccer.com/site/uploaded_files/Coaches%20Corner/Player%20Development%20versus%20Team%20Performance.pdf

126. Balyi, I., Hamilton, A. (2004) Long-Term Athlete Development: Trainability in Childhood and Adolescence Windows of Opportunity, Optimal Trainability, Victoria, National Coaching Institute British Columbia & Advanced Training and Performance Ltd, accessed online at: http://www.athleticsireland.ie/content/wp-content/uploads/2007/03/bayliLTAD2004.pdf

127. Donovan, L. In: Mahoney, R. (2002) I'm Loyal, *Soccer America*, Vol. 57(14), No. 1533, pp. 10-11, Berkeley, CA, Soccer America.

128. Ford, P. R., Yates, I., Williams, A. M. (2010) An Analysis of Practice Activities and Instructional Behaviours used by Youth Soccer Coaches during Practice: Exploring the Link between Science and Application, *Journal of Sports Sciences*, 28(5), pp. 483-495.

129. Wein, H. (2007) *Developing Youth Football Players, Tap the Full Potential of Your Young Footballers*, p. 2, Champaign, Illinois, Human Kinetics.

130. Miller, P. S., Kerr, G. A. (2002) Conceptualizing Excellence: Past, Present, and Future, *Journal of Applied Sport Psychology*, 14(3), pp. 140-153.

131. Stafford, I. (2011) *Coaching Children in Sport*, Oxon, Routledge.

132. Wenger, A. (2009) Arsenal Manager Arsene Wenger Part 2 interview, theworldgame.sbs.com.au, accessed online at: http://www.youtube.com/watch?v=NiXhHmU2VHQ&feature=relmfu

133. Whitehead, M. (2007) Physical Literacy and its Importance to Every Individual, p.12, Physical Literacy, accessed online at: http://www.physical-literacy.org.uk/dublin2007.php

134. Ford, P., De Ste Croix, M., Lloyd, R., Meyers, R., Moosavi, M., Oliver, J., et.al. (2011) The Long-Term Athlete Development Model: Physiological Evidence and Application, Journal of Sports Sciences, 29(4), pp. 389-402.

135. Balyi, I., Hamilton, A. (2004) Long-Term Athlete Development: Trainability in Childhood and Adolescence Windows of Opportunity, Optimal Trainability, Victoria, National Coaching Institute British Columbia & Advanced Training and Performance Ltd, accessed online at: http://www.athleticsireland.ie/content/wp-content/uploads/2007/03/bayliLTAD2004.pdf

136. Fenoglio, R. (2003) The Manchester United 4 V 4 Pilot Scheme for Under 9's: Part II – The Analysis, *Insight,* The FA Coaches Association Journal, 6(4), pp. 21-24, London, FA Learning.

137. Jones, S., Drust, B. (2007) Physiological and Technical Demands of 4v4 and 8v8 Games in Elite Youth Soccer Players, *Kinesiology*, 39(2), pp. 150-156.

138. Ericsson, K. A., Charness, N. (1994) Expert Performance Its Structure and Acquisition, *American Psychologist*, 49(8), pp. 725-747.

139. Helsen, W. F., Starkes, J. L., Hodges, N. J. (1998) Team Sports and the Theory of Deliberate Practice, *Journal of Sports and Exercise Psychology*, 20(1), pp. 13-35.

140. Ogden, M (2011) Manchester United manager Sir Alex Ferguson backs overhaul of academy system in bid to close gap with Barça, The Telegraph, accessed online at: http://www.telegraph.co.uk/sport/football/teams/manchester-united/8546396/Manchester-United-manager-Sir-Alex-Ferguson-backs-overhaul-of-academy-system-in-bid-to-close-gap-with-Barca.html

141. Williams, A. M., Hodges, N. J. (2005) Practice, Instruction and Skill Acquisition in Soccer: Challenging Tradition, *Journal of Sports Sciences*, 23(6), pp. 637-650.

142. Balyi, I. (2002) Long-term Athlete Development the Systems and Solutions, *Faster, Higher, Stronger*, 14(January), pp. 6-9.

143. Claxton, G., Allpress, J. (2005) Smart Coaching, *Insight*, The FA Coaches Association Journal, Autumn/Winter 2005, pp. 8-9, London, The FA Learning.

Made in the USA
San Bernardino, CA
23 May 2013